What Color is your Mountain?

A 7 WEEK DEVOTIONAL TO DISCOVER YOUR PERSPECTIVE BREAKTHROUGH WITH ART

Leesa Ward

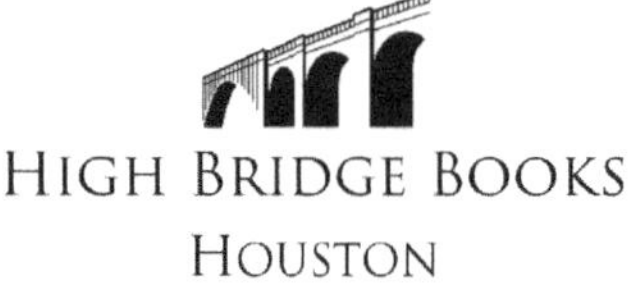

HIGH BRIDGE BOOKS
HOUSTON

What Color Is Your Mountain?
by Leesa Ward

Printed in the United States of America
ISBN: 978-1-946615-53-4

High Bridge Books titles may be purchased in bulk for educational, business, fundraising, or sales promotional use. For information, please contact High Bridge Books via www.HighBridgeBooks.com/contact.

Published in Houston, Texas by High Bridge Books.

To Kyle, my brave husband—keep conquering.

To Taylor, Annalee, and Luke, my mighty warriors—keep changing the world for Him.

To my future little legacy warriors—keep climbing.

Contents

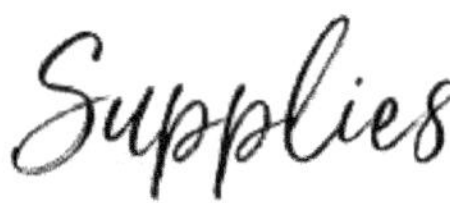

Supplies

- Winsor & Newton Cotman Watercolor Sketchers Pocket Box (includes a brush)

- 140# cold-pressed watercolor paper in either a natural or bright white

Introduction

WELCOME TO THE WORLD OF MOUNTAIN CLIMBING. The mountain's name is Perspective. We'll be looking at perspective from a daily aspect as well as from an artist's framework. The definition of perspective is a particular attitude toward or way of regarding something, a point of view. An artist's definition of perspective is the art of drawing solid objects on a two-dimensional surface to give the right impression of their height, width, depth, and position in relation to each other when viewed from a particular point. Along the journey, we will discover that you can't get to the top of the mountain unless you have just come from the valley.

We will encounter mountaintop experiences, and other times we will dwell in the valley. Still other times, we'll be singing, "She'll be comin' round the mountain" at the top of our lungs. But no matter which direction we are headed—up, down, or around the mountain—we will discover where we need to look and answer the Who, What, Where, Why, and How of the mountain Perspective.

Sometimes we need a different point of view of our current circumstances. But which point of view? Who's perspective? We are surrounded by the world's way of thinking and talking. How do we silence the voices? Each week, we will meditate on a Memory Verse, a Bible Story, a Leadership Point, and reflect and create in our journal.

Each day we will take a phrase from the Memory Verse on which to meditate. We will use the **MORE** approach to studying: **M**editate, **O**bserve, **R**epeat, and **E**xpress. We **M**editate on a phrase. We **O**bserve it in the context of the passage. We **R**epeat it or reword it in our own words. We **E**xpress it in a prayer. We will also be taking each element of art—form, shape, line, color, value, space, and texture to create your unique mixed media piece, which consists of pen and watercolors.

Being the brave one you are, we will also dig deeper in your journal time to reflect on leadership points each week to apply in our daily lives. This time is definitely an adventure that will get you out of your comfort zone. After all, what mountain climber was ever comfortable climbing into higher altitudes facing the weather and terrain? Grab your gear and enjoy the climb!

Week 1

To the Brim: What Is Perspective?

Memory Verse

> Jesus said to the servants, "Fill the jars with water"; so they filled them to the brim. Then he told them, "Now draw some out and take it to the master of the banquet." (John 2:7-8 NIV)

Leadership Concept: Capacity

Jesus fills our capacity to love to the brim so that our love can overflow onto others.

Bible Story: Jesus' Miracle of Turning Water into Wine

> On the third day a wedding took place at Cana in Galilee. Jesus' mother was there, and Jesus

and his disciples had also been invited to the wedding.

When the wine was gone, Jesus' mother said to him, "They have no more wine."

"Woman, why do you involve me?" Jesus replied. "My hour has not yet come." His mother said to the servants, "Do whatever he tells you." Nearby stood six stone water jars, the kind used by the Jews for ceremonial washing, each holding from twenty to thirty gallons. Jesus said to the servants, "Fill the jars with water"; so they filled them to the brim. Then he told them, "Now draw some out and take it to the master of the banquet." They did so, and the master of the banquet tasted the water that had been turned into wine. He did not realize where it had come from, though the servants who had drawn the water knew. Then he called the bridegroom aside and said, "Everyone brings out the choice wine first and then the cheaper wine after the guests have had too much to drink; but you have saved the best till now." What Jesus did here in Cana of Galilee was the first of the signs through which he revealed his glory; and his disciples believed in him. (John 2:1-11 NIV)

Day 1

Meditate

> Jesus said to the servants, "Fill the jars with water ... " (John 2:7 NIV)
>
> Jesus answered, "Everyone who drinks this water will be thirsty again, but whoever drinks the water I give them will never thirst. Indeed, the water I give them will become in them a spring of water welling up to eternal life."
> (John 4:13-14 NIV)

Observe

This book is about a journey up a mountain called Perspective that God has led me on for the past several years. Perspective and attitude can be used interchangeably. One's attitude is the settled way of thinking, which then gives someone their perspective or point of view. Through the next seven weeks, we will attempt to discover and apply God's perspective in our own lives and answer the six questions about it:

1. *What* is perspective?
2. *Where* do we need perspective?
3. *Why* do we need perspective?
4. *When* do we need perspective?
5. *Whose* perspective do we need?
6. And last but not least, *how* do we get perspective?

We will also be exploring and applying perspective artistically in our weekly creative challenge.

I have learned that our messes can become our messages and our tests can become our testimonies only if we choose to let them. God will work on hearts and change ways of thinking, talking, and living. Please note that there is no separation between Sunday and the rest of the week. God sets us up for great things if we are intentional about following Him every day. Part of following Him is in daily time set aside to spend with Jesus. There are no rules about what or how much time you should spend with Him, just spend it. In doing so, God fills your heart's capacity to love to a brand-new level.

In Jesus' first miracle of turning water into wine, He asked the servants to fill the jars with water. These jars were filled to their capacity. Today, He is asking us to fill our hearts and minds with the Living Water so that we will never thirst again. Filling our hearts with God's Word will keep our focus on Jesus.

The definition of capacity is the maximum amount that something can contain. Have you ever filled a glass full of water or sweet tea and there was just a little left in the pitcher? So you wanted to fit it all in the glass so as not to waste a drop. I want to be like that glass full of sweet tea. If someone touches the glass, the liquid will spill out. When someone crosses my path today, let me splash out Jesus onto the situation and conversation.

No matter your circumstances, your perspective can be higher. You can see through God's eyes. You can see others like Jesus sees them and love the unlovely. You can find out about God's character and what He says about you. You can be certain that God has written your name on a high place that will bring Him glory. After all, isn't it all about honoring the One who has carried you on this journey up the mountain? We can persevere with patience because we have an eternal perspective.

Repeat

I will see others through Jesus' eyes today.

Express

Lord, thank You for filling me with Your love. I want to spill Your love onto others today. Help me see others through Your eyes today. Help me to love like You love. In Jesus' name, amen.

Day 2

Meditate

...so they filled them to the brim. (John 2:7 NIV)

Let the words of my mouth and the meditation of my heart be acceptable in your sight, O Lord, my strength and my redeemer. (Ps. 19:14 KJV)

Observe

Each week, you will have a verse to memorize, digest, meditate on, and pray out loud each day. The acronym MORE is used to absorb and reflect on each part of the verse. Meditate. Observe. Repeat. Express. "M" is for Meditating. The original Hebrew word for meditation is *higgayown*. The literal definition is "resounding music." It's compared to the sound of the vibration a harp string makes when struck. The sound lingers and leaves the listener wanting more. It's just like being in God's Word and camping out on a verse to allow it to resonate in your soul.

Psalm 19:14 says it perfectly, "Let the words of my mouth and the meditation of my heart be acceptable in your sight, O Lord, my rock and my redeemer." It's time to slow down and think deeper into what God says about it. The enemy wants us to be so busy that we don't have time to think, just do. "**BUSY**" is the acronym for **B**eing **U**nder **S**atan's **Y**oke. Unbusy me today, Lord.

"**O**" is for **O**bserve. In this section, you will dig deeper into the context of the Scripture and apply the verse to an area and season in your life where God is working. "**R**" is for **R**epeat, to be used as your declaration throughout the day. Say this declaration out loud during the day to remind you of God's promises and truth. Faith comes by hearing, and my ears need to hear God's promises louder than the world's.

"**E**" is to **E**xpress the verse as a personal prayer. Praying God's Word is powerful. It's like reminding Him of what He has promised. When our children come to us reminding us of what we have promised, it makes us want to follow through. God wants us to honestly express all of our praise, all of our sins, all of our cares, all of our requests, and all of our love to Him. We get to choose to be filled to the brim with the Holy Spirit and overflow to others.

Repeat

I will be filled to the brim with God's love.

Express

Lord, thank You for filling me to the brim with Your love. Help me to overflow to others so that I can show them who You are. In Jesus' name, amen.

Day 3

Meditate

> Then he told them, "Now draw some out ..."
> (John 2:8 NIV)
>
> "For I know the plans I have for you," declares the Lord, "plans to prosper you and not to harm you, plans to give you hope and a future."
> (Jer. 29:11 NIV)

Observe

The Latin word *educere'* means to draw out of others through creative challenges and thinking outside the box. The verse of the week is meant to be personalized for you and your life's season, whatever or wherever that may be. Each day, you will have an additional verse to chew on. This journal is meant to be a creative way of God drawing out of you His purpose for your life.

At the end of the week, for Days 6 and 7, reflection questions are meant to allow for your creativity to journal or draw your answers to the questions. Please use all the colors you want. All of our mountains are different colors with many different paths. Our mountain doesn't have to be just one color. Your mountain may be many different shades and colors to show the world that God is so good all the time. Just know this, your mountain is beautiful and unique. God has given this journey just to you and you alone to build His kingdom and magnify His name on your mountaintop.

There will also be extra pages to journal along with each day so you can go back and remember what God did for you in this season. Each week will cover the seven elements of art: line, shape, texture, color, form, value, and space. Each of these elements can be connected to God's special plan for you. He has a special plan and purpose to draw out of you. Pay special attention to every little thing around you. Words, nature, scripture, songs ... God is talking to us everywhere. Write or draw these words and verses that keep coming to your mind as you are spending your quiet time and throughout the day. Ask yourself, "How does it all tie together?" And, by the way, He IS interested in every little detail. God is the great I AM. I am His, and He is interested.

Repeat

God has a special plan and purpose for me!

Express

Lord, thank You for giving me a special plan and purpose for my life. You are so worthy to be praised! Open my eyes to see, my ears to hear, my mind to understand, and my heart to receive everything that You have for me today. In Jesus' name, amen.

Day 4

Meditate

"...take it to the master of the banquet."
(John 2:8 NIV)

And my God will meet all your needs according to the riches of his glory in Christ Jesus.
(Phil. 4:19 NIV)

For God so loved the world that he gave his one and only Son, that whoever believes in him shall not perish but have eternal life. (John 3:16 NIV)

Observe

"Who is the Master of your banquet?" I need you to know how much I want you to accept Jesus as your Lord and Savior. I want you to have eternal life. I want you to know how much God loves you. He loves you so much that He sent His only Son to die on the cross to pay for all your sins no matter how many or how big. Sins are sins. I want you to know how to get that salvation and experience that Big Love. It's as easy as ABC:

- **A**dmit and ask for forgiveness for your sins and ask Jesus to come into your heart.
- **B**elieve Jesus came to die on the cross to pay for your sins and rose again on the third day.
- **C**onfess that Jesus is your Lord and Savior.

I want you to live an abundant life. Jesus knows each of our needs on a daily basis, and He sets a table big enough to meet those needs. I want you to RSVP to the Master's Banquet with an enthusiastic, "Yes and amen!"

Repeat

Jesus is my Lord and Savior!

Express

Lord, thank You for loving me so much that You would send Your only Son to die on the cross for my sins. I need You in my life and ask Your forgiveness of my sins. Thank You for His resurrection and everlasting love. You are my Lord and Savior. I love You too. In Jesus' name, amen.

Day 5

Meditate

> Jesus said to the servants, "Fill the jars with water"; so they filled them to the brim. Then he told them, "Now draw some out and take it to the master of the banquet." (John 2:7-8 NIV)
>
> The thief comes only to steal and kill and destroy; I have come that they may have life, and have it to the full. (John 10:10 NIV)
>
> And he said to all, "If anyone would come after me, let him deny himself and take up his cross daily and follow Me." (Luke 9:23 ESV)

Observe

God gives us the power to choose how and with what to fill our jars. Our jars are our hearts and minds. God gives us creative thoughts and ideas, which become actions and words to serve and encourage others. These thoughts can be positive or negative, helpful or harmful, life or death. We get to be aware of our thoughts and choose which ones to keep and which ones to throw away ... far, far away. Whatever is in our hearts comes out of our mouths. Let our minds and mouths be filled to the brim with thoughts that turn into life-changing words for someone. You are here to seek God's Kingdom first and serve others. Pick up your cross daily, deny yourself, and know that Jesus wants to fill your life to the brim overflowing. There is so much more.

Repeat

There is so much more!

Express

Lord, thank You for filling me to the brim with Your living water. The Best is Yet to Come! In Jesus' name, amen.

Days 6 & 7

MORE Reflection

> Jesus said to the servants, "Fill the jars with water"; so they filled them to the brim. Then he told them, "Now draw some out and take it to the master of the banquet." (John 2:7-8 NIV)

What is perspective? Perspective is reframing the situation, conversation, or attitude to be and love like Jesus. The definition of perspective in Webster's Dictionary is "a mental view or prospect." In art, perspective is what gives a three-dimensional feeling to a flat image such as a drawing or a painting. Perspective is fundamental and key to almost any drawing or sketch as well as many paintings because it creates realistic and believable scenes.

Journal

God's eternal perspective of truth and love fill my capacity of thinking about and looking at situations. To be filled "to the brim," we need our quiet time with God each day. If you are too busy for time with God, you are too busy. There are a few filter questions to ask yourself the next time you want to say yes to an activity or event.

- Does this bring peace?
- What eternal value does this have?

Create

This week's art element is *line*. Line as an element of art is defined by a point moving in space. Lines may be two-or three-dimensional, descriptive, implied, or abstract. Today, we will be using line to draw a simple drawing of a mountain range. Think about your mountaintops and your valleys as you draw your picture.

Create: Mountain Tutorial!

Gear Needed...

- pencil/pen
- Watercolor paper/journal

You will want to use at least 140 lb. weight paper that is 100% cotton and acid-free. Cold press watercolor paper has a rougher texture than hot press paper. It's just a matter of personal preference.

The Ridgeline

Draw a squiggly line going down your paper, which will be the ridgeline of the mountains. Add bumps and wiggles and allow the path to wander. Remember, we will be adding watercolor in Week 6. Your ridgeline may be painted or outlined in pen later in the drawing. I have provided an example of this line concept, but this scene is unique to you and should be what you want it to look like. Use light pencil lines at this stage in your drawing.

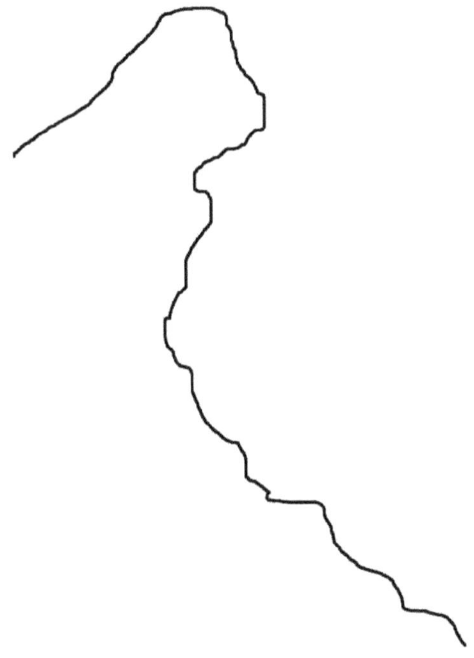

I know our mountain range looks a little empty. Don't worry—we will be adding to our mountain scene as the weeks progress using each art element. At the end of our study, we will have a masterpiece just like you!

Week 2

Hinds' Feet Wear Heels: When Do I Need Perspective?

Memory Verse

> The Lord God is my strength,
> And He has made my feet like hinds' feet,
> And makes me walk on my high places.
> (Hab. 3:19 NASB)

Leadership Concept: Commitment

God chose Habakkuk to lead His nation during troubled times. Habakkuk, whose name means "to embrace," begins his reign with wrestling questions to God about why He would allow such evil people to prosper. Then God gave him a vision of allowing an even more wicked nation to correct Judah. By the end of the book, Habakkuk is committed to trusting God and His vision with His nation's destiny. We must be committed to seeing through to the end projects, discussions, or marriages while trusting the sovereignty of God even when we don't understand or it doesn't make sense.

Bible Story: Habakkuk's Prayer

A prayer of Habakkuk the prophet. On
shigionoth.
Lord, I have heard of your fame;
I stand in awe of your deeds, Lord.
Repeat them in our day,
in our time make them known;
in wrath remember mercy.
God came from Teman,
the Holy One from Mount Paran.
His glory covered the heavens
and his praise filled the earth.
His splendor was like the sunrise;
rays flashed from his hand,
where his power was hidden.
Plague went before him;
pestilence followed his steps.
He stood, and shook the earth;
he looked, and made the nations tremble.
The ancient mountains crumbled
and the age-old hills collapsed—
but he marches on forever.
I saw the tents of Cushan in distress,
the dwellings of Midian in anguish.
Were you angry with the rivers, Lord?
Was your wrath against the streams?

Did you rage against the sea
when you rode your horses
and your chariots to victory?
You uncovered your bow,
you called for many arrows.
You split the earth with rivers;
the mountains saw you and writhed.
Torrents of water swept by;
the deep roared
and lifted its waves on high.
Sun and moon stood still in the heavens
at the glint of your flying arrows,
at the lightning of your flashing spear.
In wrath you strode through the earth
and in anger you threshed the nations.
You came out to deliver your people,
to save your anointed one.
You crushed the leader of the land of wicked-
ness, you stripped him from head to foot.
With his own spear you pierced his head
when his warriors stormed out to scatter us,
gloating as though about to devour
the wretched who were in hiding.
You trampled the sea with your horses,
churning the great waters.
I heard and my heart pounded,
my lips quivered at the sound;
decay crept into my bones,
and my legs trembled.
Yet I will wait patiently for the day of calamity
to come on the nation invading us.

Though the fig tree does not bud
  and there are no grapes on the vines,
though the olive crop fails
  and the fields produce no food,
though there are no sheep in the pen
  and no cattle in the stalls,
yet I will rejoice in the Lord,
  I will be joyful in God my Savior.
The Sovereign Lord is my strength;
  he makes my feet like the feet of a deer,
  he enables me to tread on the heights.
(Hab. 3 NIV)

Day 1

Meditate

> The Lord God is my strength...
> (Hab. 3:19 NASB)
>
> I can do all this through him who gives me strength. (Phil. 4:13 NIV)

Observe

In our hiking trip up the mountain, we can have many turns and scenic stops, such as interruptions, frustrations, and overwhelming heartaches. Or instead, they could be seen as instructions, freedom, and opportunities for happiness. It all depends on how you look at things ... what your perspective is. Your perspective could be negative or positive.

A few years ago, we traveled to the island of Maui, Hawaii. On the island, there is the legendary road to Hana, which is only 65 miles from Kahului. Nevertheless, the drive can take anywhere from two to four hours to complete since it's filled with narrow one-lane bridges, hairpin turns, as well as beautiful island views and rainforests. To be exact, the Hana Highway has 620 switchback curves and 59 bridges.

We made all the tourist stops to hike the rainforest, buy local fruit from the roadside stands, and pet the parrots. After my husband and our two oldest at the time—ages three and nine months—accomplished this round trip, we bought a t-shirt that said, "I Survived the Hana Highway." Some days I feel like I need that shirt to remind me that I am a Survivor. You are an Overcomer. You are more than a Conqueror. You are a Mighty Warrior for the Lord. Now, that's a positive perspective on the curviest of days. Today's part of the memory verse, "The Lord God is my strength..." reminds me that I more than just survive because of God's strength.

Before this verse, Habakkuk said:

> Even though the fig trees have no blossoms,
>   and there are no grapes on the vines;
> even though the olive crop fails,
>   and the fields lie empty and barren;
> even though the flocks die in the fields,
>   and the cattle barns are empty,
> yet I will rejoice in the Lord!
>   I will be joyful in the God of my salvation!
>   (Hab. 3:17-18 NLT)

Notice the progressive order of figs to livestock. It takes us from little things to big things, from luxuries to necessities, from daily circumstances to seasons. Even when things seem hopeless, and you feel helpless, God has promised that He goes before you to work things out. He is behind you to protect you and have your back. He walks beside you to carry you and hold your hand. But most importantly, He lives inside you to guide, comfort, and strengthen you.

Finding the Lord's strength is also in Philippians 4:13, "I can do all things through Christ who strengthens me." As my kids were growing up, and even now, they say the "10 Fingers" when they have to face something bravely: "I can do (fill in the blank)________(hit the ball, take the test, speak the truth) through Christ who strengthens me." The little word "all" includes good and bad, big and small, figs and cattle. These verses' context reveals that with contentment and trust in God, you will find strength.

Repeat

The Lord is my Strength all the time!

Express

Thank You, Lord, for Your strength when I am weak. Your joy is my strength. Thank You, for always being with me. Forgive me for the times I try to do it all myself. You are all I need. In Jesus' name, amen.

Day 2

Meditate

> ...And He has made my feet like hinds' feet...
> (Hab. 3:19 NASB)

Observe

In 2015, the Lord asked me to get up early to run and pray. On my early morning prayer runs, I discovered that His many critters, big and small, are out early before sunrise. In particular, on several occasions, four does crossed my path. The first time, I was terrified! Several weeks later, as the same four were crossing the road, the biggest doe stopped right in the middle of her path to look at me. We made eye contact, and it was as if God was reminding me that He is bigger and greater, yet still gentle and quiet, in this creation of His. He is in control but does not force His way on the world.

It took only a few seconds for the doe to stop and for me to slow down. Then, from out of nowhere, warm, thankful tears streamed down my face at the thought that God gave me a glimpse of His amazing power in these animals, and yet His tender love for me. On the most recent of these viewings, the verse from Habakkuk 3:19 was put on my heart immediately: "The Lord God is my strength and He has made my feet like hinds' feet and makes me walk on my high places." God was telling me that there is so much more ... or seaux much more (if you live on the bayou).

After researching "hind," I discovered the hind is a female deer whose feet can act as weapons, have exceptional tracking ability, and is of great advantage both in charging and retreating. Her back feet can be placed exactly where she places her front feet, giving her incredible balance. This ability to swiftly escape on rocky terrain from her predators is her rescue.

Is it just me or did God give us women the amazing ability of balance in the middle of topsy-turvy terrain with heels on? After all, He did promise in 1 Corinthians 10:13 (NIV), "No temptation has overtaken you except what is common to mankind. And God is faithful; he will not let you be tempted beyond what you can bear. But when you are tempted, he will also provide a way out so that you can endure it."

Just like the hind putting her back feet in the footprints of her front feet, we must keep doing our routine of Word, prayer, and fellowship when struggle and crisis come. This formula is the key to staying dependent on Christ. Keep reading your Bible plan, pray harder, be thankful, keep serving, and stay connected with your church and small group ... even when you don't feel like it. Be diligent in your routine because that is how you will be able to climb higher to your high place that God has especially for you.

The hind's feet being used as weapons is the Word you are hiding in your heart. Praying the Word is a life changer, and praying it out loud is even more life transforming because the book of James tells us to confess with our mouths.

God wants us to remind Him of His promises. He wants to know we are listening and spending time with Him. Just like our kids come to us and say, "Remember, you said...," God is ready and wants to act on those promises.

Repeat

My feet will walk in Word, prayer, and fellowship today!

Express

Thank You, Lord, for Your Word to help me fight and to comfort and guide me. Bring to mind Scripture to help me in every situation and conversation I am in today. Help me to be a light for You. In Jesus' name, amen.

Day 3

Meditate

> ...And makes me walk on my high places. (Hab. 3:19 NASB)
>
> For all those who exalt themselves will be humbled, and those who humble themselves will be exalted. (Luke 14:11 NIV)

Observe

We were made for the mountains and mountaintop views. God wants us to work, serve, and share. Don't work to retire and do nothing. Work as if you are working for the Lord and not man (Col. 3:23). The word retirement is not in the Bible. He wants us to continue our work for His Kingdom. This part of the verse promises that God has a very special and unique purpose for your life. He has a high place with your name reserved on it.

Isaiah 43:1b says, "Do not fear, for I have redeemed you; I have called you by name; you are mine!" Isaiah chapter 43 reminds us that we are called. Called to be Brave. Called to Create. Called to Love. Verse 12 gives your purpose: "So you are My witnesses." God predicted the rescue of you. Best of all, verse 13 assures us that we are called with promise. God says, "Even from eternity, I am He, and there is none who can deliver out of My hand; I act and who can reverse it?" No one can snatch you out of His hand.

As for perspective, the Bible tells us that when we exalt ourselves, He humbles us. When we humble ourselves, He exalts us. On the way to our high places, God makes His way perfect, gives us success in all our undertakings, and sets us upon our high places. He gives us both safety and dignity.

First Corinthians 1:27 says, "God chooses the foolish things of the world to shame the wise and the weak things to shame the strong" (NIV). God's economy and perspective is completely opposite of the world's.

Repeat

God will lead me to my high place!

Express

Thank You, Lord, for making me special and having a special plan just for me. Thank You for calling me by name and showing me Your ways. In Jesus' name, amen.

Day 4

Meditate

> The Lord God is my strength,
> And He has made my feet like hinds' feet,
> And makes me walk on my high places.
> (Hab. 3:19 NASB)

> The Lord is my rock, my fortress and my deliverer, my God is my rock, in whom I take refuge, my shield and the horn of my salvation, my stronghold. (Ps. 18:2 NIV)

Observe

So often, mountains are viewed as struggles, and we want God to move those mountains as soon as possible. Too quickly, we want our circumstances to become comfortable and not hurt anymore. But what if we looked at those struggling circumstances through different eyes ... God's eyes? What if we had a different perspective? Don't try to get out of these hard times prematurely. God has given you everything you need. His Spirit inside you and His Word to guide you is a window to show you when you need to change. The struggles can make us want to dig deeper and focus on Jesus. These are the times we grow and change from the inside out. You need to know how God sees you and how He wants to bless you.

The Holy Spirit has given us peace and joy. We often ask God to move our mountains, but what a perfect time to practice perspective on those mountains. What if we thought of those mountains as times to praise? Times to be thankful? What if my mountain is anywhere I am alone with God? During those quiet times, God's perspective and view are revealed to me.

Sometimes it's necessary to get above people and things you live with to be alone with God. To get to those high places, there must have just been a low place, a valley. God created us to climb the mountains, not stay in the lowlands. God's purpose is to make me in His image. On the climb up the mountain to our high place, there are plateaus, or resting places. These plateaus offer rest and renewal time to ready ourselves for the next climb or struggle. During these resting or waiting times, we may pray and ask God to change our climb or circumstance. Sometimes it's not the external circumstances that need to be changed but instead my heart that needs to change. These plateaus are times for me to set my mind and heart on God and keep climbing.

It's important not to get out of our struggles prematurely because God is using this climb to mature us and help us grow in our faith. Get comfortable in the uncomfortable. Just know that the best is yet to come and the High Place is just around the corner. Choose to live by faith demonstrated by your actions. Faith is acting on what we believe to be true about God. By spending time in Word, Prayer, and Fellowship, we get to know the true character of God. Trust is a choice and a process.

Repeat

I choose to keep climbing because God is growing me!

Express

Thank You, Lord, for my struggles that help me grow. You know the big picture and what is best for me. Nothing comes into my life without You allowing it or causing it to happen. You waste nothing. You are in control. Thank You, Lord. In Jesus' name, amen.

Day 5

Meditate

The Lord God is my strength,
And He has made my feet like hinds' feet,
And makes me walk on my high places.
(Hab. 3:19 NASB)

He makes my feet like hinds' feet
and sets me on my high places.
(2 Sam. 22:34 NASB)

In the NLT translation, the same verse reads:

He makes me as surefooted as a deer,
enabling me to stand on mountain heights.

He makes my feet like hinds' feet,
And sets me upon my high places.
(Ps. 18:33 NASB)

When things are important, they're worth repeating. When God repeats anything in the Bible, it's time to sit up and listen carefully because you know it's important. These three verses are almost all identical in their wording.

Observe

David was a musician who composed and performed his original hits for kings. In Psalm 18:33, David wrote this song of praise toward the end of his life retelling God's rescue of David from a giant, Saul and his merry men chasing him in the mountains, backsliding, Israel's enemies, Absalom, and his adultery with Bathsheba and murder of her husband, Uriah. Often, when I have been relieved or relented from hard times, my first response is to prove the naysayers wrong and take full credit of all the good that has come out of the situation. But what if we could recognize the need for praise and worship to the God who worked it all out, to point to Him and exalt Him as our first response?

David's song was a praise and worship song with a driving beat that gave God every ounce of credit where credit was due. It was quite possibly one of the earliest "rock" songs because it starts with loud voices exclaiming, "The Lord is my Rock, my fortress, and my savior." Then, in verse 32, "For who is God except the Lord? Who but our God is a solid rock?" He sang this song with confidence that the Lord is his strength and has a special purpose for his life. May we be that confident to sing our praises to the Lord who has saved us from the world's darkness. We are made in His image, and we are new creatures who are walking on high places.

Repeat

> I am a new creature who is walking on high places.

Express

Thank You, Lord, for making me fearfully and wonderfully made. Thank You for setting me on my high places for You. In Jesus' name, amen.

Days 6 & 7

MORE Reflection

> The Lord God is my strength,
> And He has made my feet like hinds' feet,
> And makes me walk on my high places.
> (Hab. 3:19 NASB)

When do you need perspective? You need perspective when the world's reasoning and view tries to override commitment to Christ.

Journal

Habakkuk asked God some really hard questions about a dying and dark world. He saw evil everywhere. He saw the wicked winning. God answered Habakkuk with a multitude of evidence that His presence is in the world and hope is on the way.

This week's journal is a picture of a hind's foot. On the left side of the foot, list a current or past struggle, and on the right side, comment on how God stretched you or is stretching you through this situation. In the middle, on the hind's foot, write the verse you held onto during this growth opportunity.

Hind's Foot

Struggle Scripture Stretch

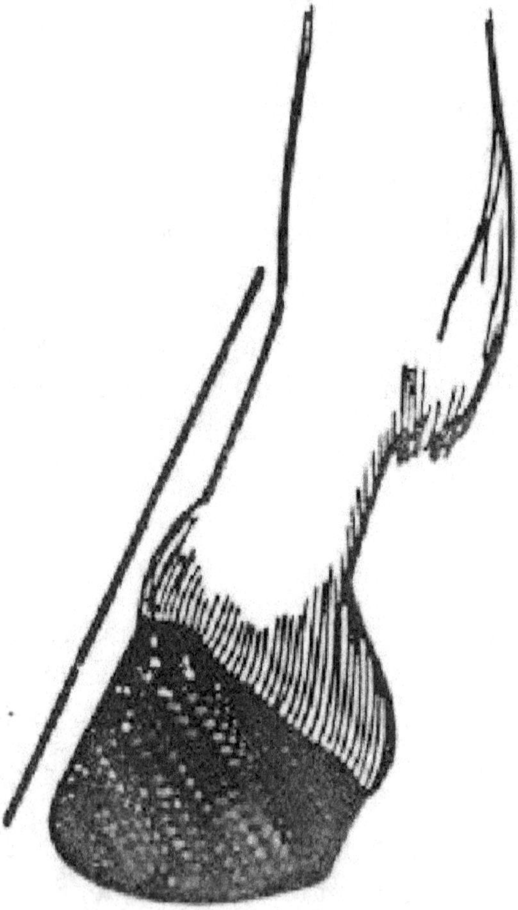

Fig. 2

What do you do during the plateaus or resting and waiting periods when you feel confused about what God is doing or not doing? Not all the questions can be answered neatly wrapped up and tied with a bow. Some questions create more questions. In searching for answers, doubts can come and hearts can become hardened, or we can choose to trust God's sovereignty and celebrate that He is the One in charge in the world.

1. He wants us to be honest with Him. Tell Him you feel confused. Tell Him you feel frustrated. Tell Him you feel sad. God understands how you feel—don't apologize for it—and He wants to be in your presence and help change the way you think. Remember, He is always with us and knows us better than we know ourselves.
2. Ask God to open your ears to hear what He has for you. Listen and really hear what the Lord says. Pay attention to certain words that keep coming up in conversations and your quiet time. Write them. Draw them. Remember, God talks to us through others, Scripture, and nature. Plan margin into your busy day to really be able to listen and be sensitive to the Holy Spirit.
3. Receive and Believe. Speak it out loud. Speak life into that promise you are camping out on today. Speak it over your family or friends today.

Create

Form as an art element is a three-dimensional shape. Form has length, width, and depth. Like our relationships, let's go below the surface with each other. Be vulnerable. Be real. Our friendships and relationships deserve depth. This week's art element is Form, which is a shape in three dimensions. So, let's add to our mountains.

Add Slopes

With the ridgeline in place from Week 1, take lines off from the angles in the ridgeline to make your path and plateaus. Basically, anywhere your ridgeline changes direction, you can draw a ridge coming off. These should be steeper near the crest and smooth out toward the edge to show sharp peaks.

Days 6 & 7

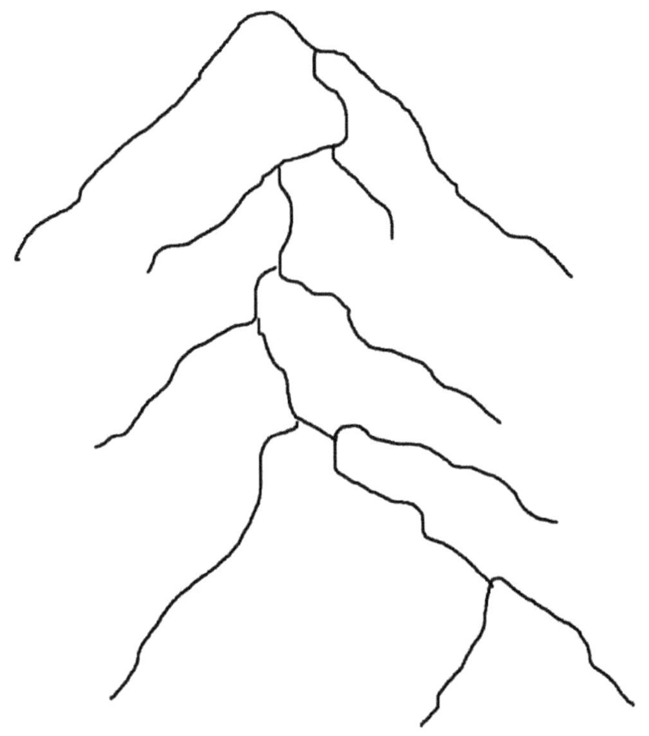

Week 3

The King of My Mountain: Whose Perspective Is Needed?

Memory Verse for the Week:

> The Lord said, "Go out and stand on the mountain in the presence of the Lord, for the Lord is about to pass by." (1 Kgs 19:11 NIV)

Leadership Quality: Empowerment

God empowers Elijah and us to be world changers.

Bible Story: Elijah on the Mountain

> Now Ahab told Jezebel everything Elijah had done and how he had killed all the prophets with the sword. So Jezebel sent a messenger to Elijah to say, "May the gods deal with me, be it ever so severely, if by this time tomorrow I do not make your life like that of one of them."

Elijah was afraid and ran for his life. When he came to Beersheba in Judah, he left his servant there, while he himself went a day's journey into the wilderness. He came to a broom bush, sat down under it, and prayed that he might die. "I have had enough, Lord," he said. "Take my life; I am no better than my ancestors." Then he lay down under the bush and fell asleep.

All at once an angel touched him and said, "Get up and eat." He looked around, and there by his head was some bread baked over hot coals, and a jar of water. He ate and drank and then lay down again.

The angel of the Lord came back a second time and touched him and said, "Get up and eat, for the journey is too much for you." So he got up and ate and drank. Strengthened by that food, he traveled forty days and forty nights until he reached Horeb, the mountain of God. There he went into a cave and spent the night.

And the word of the Lord came to him: "What are you doing here, Elijah?"

He replied, "I have been very zealous for the Lord God Almighty. The Israelites have rejected your covenant, torn down your altars, and put your prophets to death with the sword. I am the only one left, and now they are trying to kill me too."

The Lord said, "Go out and stand on the mountain in the presence of the Lord, for the Lord is about to pass by."

Then a great and powerful wind tore the mountains apart and shattered the rocks before the Lord, but the Lord was not in the wind. After the wind there was an earthquake, but the Lord was not in the earthquake. After the earthquake came a fire, but the Lord was not in the fire. And after the fire came a gentle whisper. When Elijah heard it, he pulled his cloak over his face and went out and stood at the mouth of the cave.

Then a voice said to him, "What are you doing here, Elijah?"

He replied, "I have been very zealous for the Lord God Almighty. The Israelites have rejected your covenant, torn down your altars, and put your prophets to death with the sword. I am the only one left, and now they are trying to kill me too."

The Lord said to him, "Go back the way you came, and go to the Desert of Damascus. When you get there, anoint Hazael king over Aram. Also, anoint Jehu son of Nimshi king over Israel, and anoint Elisha son of Shaphat from Abel Meholah to succeed you as prophet. Jehu will put to death anyone who escapes the sword of Hazael, and Elisha will put to death anyone who escapes the sword of Jehu. Yet I reserve seven thousand in Israel—all whose knees have not bowed down to Baal and whose mouths have not kissed him."

So Elijah went from there and found Elisha, son of Shaphat. He was plowing with twelve yoke of oxen, and he himself was driving the twelfth pair. Elijah went up to him and threw his cloak around him. Elisha then left his oxen and ran after Elijah. "Let me kiss my father and mother goodbye," he said, "and then I will come with you."

"Go back," Elijah replied. "What have I done to you?"

So Elisha left him and went back. He took his yoke of oxen and slaughtered them. He burned the plowing equipment to cook the meat and gave it to the people, and they ate. Then he set out to follow Elijah and became his servant. (1 Kgs. 19 NIV)

Day 1

Meditate

"Go out..." (1 Kgs. 19:11 NIV)

So go and make followers of all people in the world. Baptize them in the name of the Father and the Son and the Holy Spirit.
(Matt. 28:19 NCV)

Observe

Jesus specifically commands and empowers us in Matthew 28:19-20, "Go out into the world and make disciples, preaching the gospel." During the summer of 2017, my family and I had the awesome opportunity to travel to Madagascar, Africa, on a mission trip with SOS Adventures and our local church to love people to Jesus. The beautiful Malagasy people are so grateful and happy while immersed in poverty and filth. The amazing desperateness in their faith to absorb the gospel like a sponge and experience the miracles of Jesus is beyond refreshing. I want that same desperateness, that same simplicity, that same contentedness.

But you don't have to travel halfway around the world to obey Christ's command and see miracles. All you have to do is walk out your door to your workplace, school, or grocery store, or even stay in your house doing laundry and housework for your family. Wherever you are in life or season, you have the awesome job of sharing Jesus with everyone around you in your little corner of the world. You can serve and share with others with both words and actions. Your actions sometimes speak louder than words.

Repeat

I will go out and share the good news today in my corner of the world.

Express

Father, I praise You today for sending your Son to die on the cross and forgiving me for my sins so that I can have eternal life. I thank You, Lord, for the abundant life I can have here on earth. Lord, make me desperate today and open my eyes to see all the opportunities to share the good news and Your love. Break my heart for what breaks Yours. Help me to share the good news of the abundant life you want us to experience today. In Jesus' name, amen.

Day 2

Meditate

... and stand on the mountain...
(1 Kgs. 19:11 NIV)

Truly I tell you, if anyone says to this mountain, "Go, throw yourself into the sea," and does not doubt in their heart but believes that what they say will happen, it will be done for them.
(Mark 11:23 NIV)

Observe

In recent years, our family has enjoyed several Christmases in Jackson Hole, Wyoming. The first year, we flew on December 23rd. We were scheduled to arrive at 8:15 p.m. After flying in a holding pattern over the Jackson Hole airport for 45 minutes, the pilot decided to take us to Salt Lake City, Utah. We were given hotel vouchers but not our luggage.

During the shuttle ride to the hotel, we met a lady, Betty, who was also traveling to Jackson Hole to spend the holidays with her grandchildren. We became instant friends, not knowing about our future adventure. We were given reboarding instructions, but no dinner, to be back in the hotel lobby the next morning at 5:30 a.m. to catch the shuttle back to the airport.

So, to say the least, we were traveling with "hangry" teenagers. My husband and I were both reading Joyce Meyer's *The Battlefield of the Mind*. Just let me say that you will be empowered to practice the things you are reading and studying. And, boy, did we ever get the practice to "think about what you're thinking about" and stay positive during this situation. We definitely received the answer to the question, "Whose perspective do we need right now?" This delay could be seen as a huge interruption for my to-do list of grocery shopping and Christmas prep a thousand miles away from home. Who needed that hassle? But what if we subscribed to God's plan of changing the world through our delays and our destruction of our to-do lists.

After a night of sleeping in our clothes and brushing our teeth with a toothbrush from the front desk, we met in the hotel lobby as directed at 5:30 a.m. sharp. After reboarding the plane in Salt Lake City and doing another holding pattern above Jackson Hole for an hour, the pilot announced that due to inclement weather, he was returning to Salt Lake City to leave us on our own accord to get home or get to our final desired location of Jackson Hole, Wyoming for Christmas.

To say the least, there was a mutiny on the ship, or, in this case, the plane. The airline planned to take us back to DFW airport and be done with us. Oh no, the Wards were not going to be satisfied with that solution. So we debarked the plane, demanded our luggage, and set off to find the transportation for the next leg of our journey. After discovering the shuttle bus was sold out and all rental cars were rented, the only other option was a taxi.

Remember our friend Betty? We ran into her again and offered to include her in our mode of transportation, whatever that may be at this point. In her relief, she happily accepted our invitation. Even in not being sure of how she was getting to where she was going, she was at least happy to be included and accepted by her new family. Does that sound like someone you know, who includes and accepts you just as you are?

Little did we know that our Christmas angel was a Somalian man named Nor. Six hours later and several dollars in the meter, Nor drove us through ice and snow, a real-life cattle drive, and an irate phone call from his wife on Christmas Eve, only to have to make the return trip alone in the dark. Nor sacrificed his time and Christmas to get us to where we wanted to go. He was our Christmas miracle.

What if our prayers every morning sounded something like this, "Lord, make me a blessing to someone today. Use me today. I'm on Your schedule today." Needless to say, blessings abounded, as we arrived in the Teton Mountain Range surrounding Jackson Hole, Wyoming, safely. The taxi driver, Nor, also known as a Christmas angel, delivered a grandma to her family, and our family to its final destination. Hopefully, we were able to reciprocate as a blessing to him and his family. It was truly a Christmas miracle on all fronts that year.

Hills and mountains are mentioned more than 500 times in the Bible. Christian and Jewish cultures have symbolized mountains as being places closer to God, who often revealed Himself on mountaintops. On Mount Sinai, God made a covenant with Moses and presented to him the 10 Commandments. There is the Sermon on the Mount (Beatitudes), the Mount of Olives, Mount Zion, Mount Tabor where the Transfiguration took place, Mount Carmel where Elijah challenges Baal prophets to see whose god could ignite a fire, just to name a few.

Mountains can symbolize easy climbs and steep uphill battles. Sometimes in our lives, the journey up the mountains symbolizes betrayal, brokenness, and broken hearts. As David was running from his son Absalom's betrayal, he climbed the Mount of Olives in 2 Samuel 15:30. David was "weeping as he went." In Psalm 3:7, David cried out to God, "Arise, O Lord! Save me, O my God!" while standing on the Mount of Olives. Interestingly enough, Jesus climbed the same mountain, physically and figuratively, on the night of his betrayal before His last breath. Both men were weeping, both men were betrayed, both men prayed to God to rescue them.

God hears our cries and holds every tear in his hand. I have seen God move those betrayal mountains, those addiction mountains, those heart-broken mountains, and I believe He will again. When we want Him to move the mountain, we are in the valley, but we can be hopeful and confident that He will help us to become strong mountain climbers. God will help us climb the mountain and stand on the mountaintop.

Repeat

I have seen You move mountains, and I believe
You will help me stand on the mountaintop!

Express

Dear Lord, I thank You for the mountains in my life that I am asking You to move, because I know You are with me and making me stronger every day. I am growing in Your love and grace to bring glory to Your name. Lord, make me a blessing to someone today. Use me today. I'm on Your schedule today. In Jesus' name, amen!

Day 3

Meditate

> ... in the presence of the Lord...
> (1 Kgs. 19:11 NIV)
>
> No power in the sky above or in the earth below—indeed, nothing in all creation will ever be able to separate us from the love of God that is revealed in Christ Jesus our Lord.
> (Rom. 8:39 NLT)

Observe

How do you feel the presence of the Lord? Is it a feeling? Is it a physical change? It can be either, but so often it's just knowing and feeling that peace that surpasses all understanding in the middle of chaos. Sometimes God sends winks to us through the smallest of things. During a time of loss and helplessness in the cold winter, He sent ladybugs by the coffee pot to me. During that same season, two doves lingered on my front porch, reminding me of God's overflowing peace. Shooting stars and four does meet me on my early morning prayer and amaze me with God's power and control of everything around me.

About three years ago, the Lord asked me to get up early to take a prayer run. I feel His presence on these runs, and I actually hear from God during this time. Prayer is opening up communication between you and God. It is a two-way conversation. We must be aware of everything around us daily. Whether it be in nature, conversations, circumstances, and in reading the Word, God speaks to us in all these ways. The Bible begins and ends with God's presence in a beautiful garden.

In Genesis, the Garden of Eden was created for Adam and Eve to enjoy God's presence. At the end of the Bible in Revelation, God's promise of a new earth in His eternal presence is revealed. We cannot separate our weekdays from our Sundays, just like nothing can separate us from God's love. We can feel God's presence if we choose to focus on Him every day. The hat we wear to work should be the same hat we wear to church, with no separation from God's love. So why would I want to separate my life from God's presence?

Repeat

I choose to stay in the presence of God and see all of His winks today!

Express

Dear Lord, thank You for Your promise that nothing can separate Your love from me. Help me to feel Your presence in every part of my day today. Help my family feel Your arms around them today! In Jesus' name, amen!

Day 4

Meditate

> ... for the Lord is about to pass by.
> (1 Kgs. 19:11 NIV)
>
> And we know that God causes everything to work together for the good of those who love God and are called according to his purpose for them. (Rom. 8:28 NLT)

Observe

The phrase "for the Lord is about to pass by" speaks of so much expectation and confidence that the Lord WILL pass by. How comforting to know that the Lord will show up, and He will not be late. But how will the Lord pass by? What do we need to look for to know it's Him? That question was asked on that night in the barn with a manger, a dirty, handmade, hay-filled manger. A dirty barn? That's what the Jews were wondering in Jerusalem as Jesus was entering the city on a donkey. A little donkey? And what about that devastating day when it all went dark and the veil was torn. A wooden cross?

The Lord always shows up in the most unexpected, sweet, and powerful ways. He does not want us to rely on our own plans for Him to show up and work things out because He knows we would want to take the credit. He is building His Kingdom in the craziest of ways. He shows up in the whispers and winks. Be confident in His promise that He is working things out for the good for those who love Him and are called for His purpose.

After 40 days of being in the wilderness and hiking up the mountain, Elijah was hiding out in a cave in a mountain having a pity party at his lowest point. He had just spent 40-plus days wallowing in his own thoughts and problems; Elijah had lost touch with God. He expected God to come in a wind, earthquake, and fire. But, no, none of these things ... God came in a whisper. God's whisper empowered Elijah to empower Elisha to become Elijah's predecessor as prophet. Elijah was a mighty man of God who was tired but knew God's presence was always with Him and working things out for His glory.

Repeat

I will expect You to work things out for the good because I love You!

Express

Dear Lord, thank You for working things out for the good that builds Your kingdom. I trust you to pass by in Your perfect timing and ways. Empower me to be Your mouthpiece and hands and feet. In Jesus' name, amen!

Day 5

Meditate

> The Lord said, "Go out and stand on the mountain in the presence of the Lord, for the Lord is about to pass by." (1 Kgs. 19:11 NIV)

Observe

Elijah had just won the "Battle of the Prophets" by asking God to burn up his wet sacrifices in front of a crowd. The evil queen, Jezebel, had a bounty out for Elijah because he had humiliated her prophet friends. So Elijah ran to the wilderness and wanted to die. Do you think Elijah felt lonely, discouraged, or unmotivated? God knew just how Elijah felt, so He sent angels to feed and care for Elijah. The Old Testament has a red thread running through the pages to ultimately tie it to the blood of Jesus saving us in the New Testament.

Like Elijah, Jesus was also tempted in the desert for 40 days. God provided for Elijah before he endured his 40 days in the desert. Jesus endured the desert first and then God sent angels to Him to provide nourishment just like Elijah. So often, we want to see big signs from God that He is working. We want to see things like earthquakes, tornadoes, and volcanoes so we know God is taking care of the situation. We want to see immediate and mighty works. But God wants us to get away from the chaos. Step away from the situation and try to see the big picture. Find a place all by yourself and pray just like Jesus did many times during His time here on earth. Stand back and just listen to the small whispers around you. God is not a God of chaos. He is a God of order and depends on us to do our part to keep that peace. Protect your margin and downtime. That is when God is talking to us. Trust in God and not the plan we think God should follow. God's plans don't have to match our plans for them to still be good. In fact, our plans don't usually coincide. Usually, they collide and the Lord leads you back to the wilderness to give you His perspective and faith.

Repeat

> Today I will get alone with You, Lord, to hear Your whispers.

Express

> Lord, I thank You for Your presence. Thank You for your peace. Thank You for your compassion and mercy. In Jesus' name, amen.

Days 6 & 7

MORE Reflection

The Lord said, "Go out and stand on the mountain in the presence of the Lord, for the Lord is about to pass by." Then a great and powerful wind tore the mountains apart and shattered the rocks before the Lord, but the Lord was not in the wind. After the wind there was an earthquake, but the Lord was not in the earthquake. (1 Kgs. 19:11 NIV)

For I know the thoughts that I think toward you, saith the LORD, thoughts of peace, and not of evil, to give you an expected end. (Jer. 29:11 KJV)

The mountains quake before him
   and the hills melt away.
The earth trembles at his presence,
   the world and all who live in it.
(Nah. 1:5 NIV)

> I lift up my eyes to the mountains—
>   where does my help come from?
> My help comes from the LORD,
>   the Maker of heaven and earth.
> (Ps. 121:1-2 NIV)

Whose perspective is needed? Empowerment is the authority or power given to someone to do something. God empowers us to make a difference in someone's life.

Journal

God loves to ask questions. In 1 Kings 19:9, He asked, "What are you doing here, Elijah?" God also asked Adam this question in the Garden of Eden after he and Eve ate the fruit, asking, "Where are you?" In the New Testament, in Mark 5:25-34, Jesus asked who touched Him from the crowd. It was the woman who had bled for 12 years. Don't you think God knew where Adam and Elijah were? After all, God is omniscient, which means He is all knowing all the time.

He asked these location questions of Elijah and Adam and then asks them of us to give us an opportunity to be honest with ourselves and with Him—which is, by the way, one of the hardest things to do. God is asking you right now, "Where are you? What are you doing here? Where are you on the mountain right now? Are you climbing? Are you on a plateau? Are you on the mountaintop? What will you do next? Will you trust Me? Will you let Me heal you? Will you let Me lead you? Will you follow Me?"

Create

This week's art element is *value,* which is the darkness or lightness of a color. Adding value to your drawing adds realistic features. I've laid in shadows with some basic hatching. Hatching is lines either parallel or crossing. You can decide how you want to add value to your object by using the different techniques of shading. You can shade by cross-hatching (diagonal lines), hatching (parallel lines), blending, scribbling (doodles), and stippling (small dots). Examples of shading are included to give you ideas.

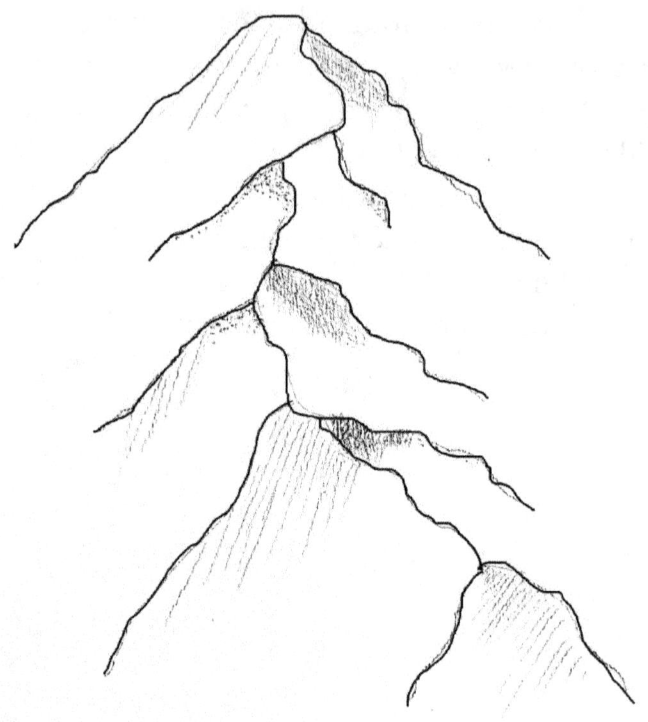

hatching

cross hatching

stippling

scribbling

Use lines far apart for a lighter shadow and closer hatching for deeper shadows. Keep your deeper/darker shadows to the top of the ridgeline (where it's steepest) and in valleys and crevasses.

Week 4

View from the Top: Where Is Perspective?

Memory Verse:

> Then Mary took about a pint of pure nard, an expensive perfume; she poured it on Jesus' feet and wiped his feet with her hair. And the house was filled with the fragrance of the perfume. (John 12:3 NIV)

Leadership: Intentional

We must be intentional with our giving, our serving, our growing, and especially our praise and worship. We grow intentionally by filling our minds with Scripture, books, music, and podcasts. Mary was intentional with her praise and worship of Jesus.

Bible Story: Mary Anoints Jesus

Six days before the Passover, Jesus came to Bethany, where Lazarus lived, whom Jesus had raised from the dead. Here a dinner was given in Jesus' honor. Martha served, while Lazarus was among those reclining at the table with him. Then Mary took about a pint of pure nard, an expensive perfume; she poured it on Jesus' feet and wiped his feet with her hair. And the house was filled with the fragrance of the perfume.

But one of his disciples, Judas Iscariot, who was later to betray him, objected, "Why wasn't this perfume sold and the money given to the poor? It was worth a year's wages." He did not say this because he cared about the poor but because he was a thief; as keeper of the money bag, he used to help himself to what was put into it.

"Leave her alone," Jesus replied. "It was intended that she should save this perfume for the day of my burial. You will always have the poor among you, but you will not always have me." (John 12:1-8 NIV)

Day 1

Meditate

> Then Mary took about a pint of pure nard, an expensive perfume… (John 12:3 NIV)
>
> And the peace of God, which surpasses all understanding, will guard your hearts and your minds in Christ Jesus. (Phil. 4:7 ESV)
>
> The thief comes only to steal and kill and destroy; I have come that they may have life, and have it to the full. (John 10:10 NIV)

Observe

To set the stage of Mary's act of affection, it is six days before Passover. The religious leaders are plotting the arrest and death of Jesus. Sisters Mary and Martha and their brother Lazarus have prepared a dinner in Jesus' honor. Sweet-spirited Mary decided to anoint Jesus' feet with a very special oil, nard. Pure nard is a small aromatic plant that grows in the Himalayan Mountains, which makes it very valuable. The oil extracted from the nard plant is worth at least 300 denarii, which is about a whole year's wages for an ordinary laborer.

Mary was intentional with her expensive perfume and her worship of Jesus. She held nothing back in her praise and worship. Mary had joy and peace during this time of tension before Jesus' death. She was intentional in not letting Judas steal her joy and peace. We can also be intentional and decide right now that no one will steal that peace and joy today.

Perspective is when we choose to see through God's eyes and experience the peace that no one can understand. Yes, we must face reality but then remember what God wants to do with our hard times. He wants to make us more like Jesus. So speak over that circumstance and believe that God will work things out for the good of those who love Him and who are called for His purpose. The view from the top of the mountain is beautiful and peaceful. I choose to name my mountain *Perspective*.

Repeat

> I will find the joy and peace God has given me today!

Express

> Lord, thank You for giving me your joy and peace that surpasses all understanding. I choose not to let anyone steal my joy and peace today with Your strength. In Jesus' name, amen.

Day 2

Meditate

> ...she poured it on Jesus' feet... (John 12:3 NIV)
>
> I am the vine; you are the branches. If you remain in me and I in you, you will bear much fruit; apart from me you can do nothing.
> (John 15:5 NIV)
>
> Now to him who is able to do immeasurably more than all we ask or imagine, according to his power that is at work within us...
> (Eph. 3:20 NIV)

Observe

The alabaster jar that contained the expensive nard had a narrow neck that could be sealed to measure the perfume in effective amounts. Keep in mind that just a few days before, Mary had just seen Jesus raise her brother from the dead. So Mary was so excited to share the perfume with Jesus that she poured the entire bottle on His feet. She did not spill the perfume. She intentionally poured the oil to anoint

Jesus. The entire house was filled with the aromatic fragrance of the luxurious oil.

Among the partygoers was Judas Iscariot, who selfishly corrected Mary for the wasteful use of the perfume. The sale of the perfume could have helped the poor. God can do abundantly above and beyond all we could ever ask for or imagine. He wants to bless us so that we can pour into others. The abundant life is so much more than just things. It is living in freedom from the way the world works and thinks.

People and life become very messy. You may ask yourself, "How do I find myself in such a mess?" What is the real root of addictions, divorce, brokenness? Selfishness, anger, bitterness, rejection, resentment, and jealousy are all feeder roots that need to be cut as soon as they appear. The vine we need to be attached to is Jesus. We must be intentional about remaining in Him through reading the Bible and praying. A great place to start is with the gospel of John. Another idea for a Bible reading routine is reading five Psalms a day. There are 31 days in most months and 31 Proverbs. So you could read the Proverb that corresponds to the month's date and finish all 150 Psalms by reading 5 per day during any given month.

But, no, the enemy wants us to think we have it under control. Instead, the weeds of resentment grow longer and deeper. They want to tie you up and make you numb. Reflection and identification about yourself can be very difficult. You want to stay on the surface. Don't let anyone get too close in relationships. Don't go too deep because they may see who you really are and what you've really let happen. Don't get discovered because then you would have to feel more shame and rejection. Things are taken way too personally. We get offended. These lies are exactly what the enemy wants us to think.

When we realize that the little devil is only about 18 inches tall and all we have to do is flick him off our shoulder, spit in his face, and stomp on him, life will be abundant. God wants us to remain or abide in Him only. The word "abide" means to stay, to keep on, and to remain and expect something in the future. Abiding is both unhurried and active. Choose today to believe in the confident hope in Jesus Christ and abide.

Repeat

I know that the best is yet to come!

Express

Lord, I believe today that You are able to do abundantly above and beyond. You want me to stay in Your Word and follow Your ways. In Jesus' name, amen.

Day 3

Meditate

> ...and wiped his feet with her hair.
> (John 12:3 NIV)

> He determines the number of the stars;
>   he gives to all of them their names.
> Great is our Lord, and abundant in power;
>   his understanding is beyond measure.
> (Ps. 147:4-5 ESV)

Observe

About three years ago, the Lord asked me to get up at 4:30 a.m. to pray while I ran. It had to be the Lord to ask me to get up that early. Sometimes you have to be intentional about being obedient, like setting an alarm. I'm a runner for two reasons: It is cheaper than therapy, and I love to eat, especially chocolate sweet things. Early morning calorie burning runs also offers a great view of the beauty of a million stars twinkling in the sky. It is truly overwhelming. And to think that God has named every last one of them is amazing. Being able to view His creation from this time of the day really puts His control of the universe in perspective. Who am I who He loves so much to have sent His son to die on the cross to forgive my sins and want to live with me for eternity? His ways and thoughts are higher than mine, and He is in control of everything. His timing is perfect and not one season we go through is wasted.

Repeat

I am amazed at God's power all around me!

Express

Lord, thank You for preparing me for the next season today. It is Your power that I trust and will never let me down. Thank You for Your amazing power working in me to love others to Jesus! In Jesus' name, amen.

Day 4

Meditate

> And the house was filled… (John 12:3 NIV)
>
> And I am certain that God, who began the good work within you, will continue his work until it is finally finished on the day when Christ Jesus returns. (Phil. 1:6 NLT)

Observe

During the holidays, my house is filled with aromas of favorite dishes both sweet and unsweet. It also gets filled with friends and family who come from different backgrounds and geographics. Several years ago, my husband and I purchased an oak farm table. When the delivery guys set up the table, they put the two leaves in it. The table could seat ten people. The next day, someone asked me if I was going to leave the table so big. "Of course! I want to fill this table up as often as I can," I replied.

To fill that table and my house, I would need to plan and prepare some serious meals. I would need to work in the kitchen and work on building relationships with people who would want to sit at my table. Gathering around a table is a special time of conversation and board game playing. It is a time to sit face to face and next to each other to work things out. Jesus sets a table for each one of us every day with exactly what we need. What part of you is God working on today?

Times of struggle or heartache are opportunities to be more like Jesus. These times can be called "growing seasons." This season is the "good work" that Paul talks about in this verse. It may not feel good right now, but it will produce good results like learning to love like Jesus, growing closer to Jesus, and seeing through His eyes. Stay in the present for the in-between times. God begins His good work, and He is faithful to complete it. He will never leave us in the waiting times. We must give ourselves to Him every day in quiet time. Christ works in us to show Christ through us. In other words, the internal reality produces external evidence.

Repeat

I will be intentional to fill my table today.

Express

Lord, thank You for setting a table for me today. I know You are working in me right now. Give me Your strength to remember and hold onto the confidence, knowing that You are working everything out for the good. I love You! In Jesus' name, amen.

Day 5

Meditate

> ...with the fragrance of the perfume.
> (John 12:3 NIV)
>
> For we are a fragrance of Christ to God among those who are being saved and among those who are perishing... (2 Cor. 2:15 NASB)
>
> Therefore be imitators of God, as beloved children; and walk in love, just as Christ also loved you and gave Himself up for us, an offering and a sacrifice to God as a fragrant aroma.
> (Eph. 5:1-2 NASB)
>
> Oil and perfume make the heart glad,
> So a man's counsel is sweet to his friend.
> (Prov. 27:9 NASB)

Observe

Often in the Old Testament, clouds symbolized God's presence. The fragrance of perfume fills the room with its sweet smells. God's presence fills our lives with His sweet grace and mercy. Where do you need God's perspective and presence in your life? We need His wisdom and perspective in every situation. James tells us that if we ask for wisdom and ask for it without doubt, we will receive it. *I believe. Lord, help my unbelief.* Believe God will give you a double portion of wisdom. Wisdom helps you to have God's perspective and see people and situations from His eyes of grace. The sweet aroma of wisdom is knowledge and understanding at work with a pure heart and motives.

God's power to create the earth and hold it together with His infinite wisdom is amazing to think about. And then on top of that, He loved and thought enough of you to make you. You are loved, adored, and accepted by your Father in heaven. He calls you His masterpiece. Be overwhelmed by God's perspective and be sensitive to His presence in His amazing creation.

Repeat

I am God's sweet-smelling masterpiece.

Express

Thank You for being a God who wants to answer big prayers in a big way. Let Your power work through me to love like You do. Give me Your sweet perfume of wisdom to share with others today. In Jesus' name, amen.

Days 6 & 7

MORE Reflection

> Then Mary took about a pint of pure nard, an expensive perfume; she poured it on Jesus' feet and wiped his feet with her hair. And the house was filled with the fragrance of the perfume. (John 12:3 NIV)

Where is your perspective? We must be intentional to find God's perspective in our every day.

Journal

Mary intentionally poured the sweet perfume on Jesus' feet and then wiped His feet with her hair. She knew that Jesus was more than enough for her. She knew Jesus would provide for her needs. The least she could do was share the expensive fragrance with Him. The real question here is, "Do I really *believe* that God is able to do immeasurably more than all I ask or imagine?" I try to put God in a box. I approach Him thinking He has limits. But He does not. He is a big God. He is a God of Miracles ... big miracles. So why don't we pray big prayers. He wants us to pray those big prayers. He's ready to answer those prayers that are more than we could ever imagine. Keep in mind that God is not a Genie in a bottle. Start praying for internal change to get external results.

God is able ... am I available? Yes, I am available NOW—there is No Other Way to be. Trust God to be big in His answers. Trust is faith in action, which produces fruit. God's love gives us the power to love the unlovely. Sometimes we must pour out our hearts with praise and worship to uncover our heart and surrender to God what is already His.

Journal a ridiculously big prayer today.

Create

Our creative project this week is about texture. In the visual arts, texture is the perceived surface quality of a work of art. It is an element that can be two-dimensional and three-dimensional designs and is distinguished by its perceived visual and physical properties. Use of texture, along with other elements of design, can convey a variety of messages and emotions. We can add texture to our mountain range by adding more value and directional markings. You can extend your ridges. Be intentional with your markings. Think about where your light source is and add more shadows and highlights with circular shading.

Day 6 & 7

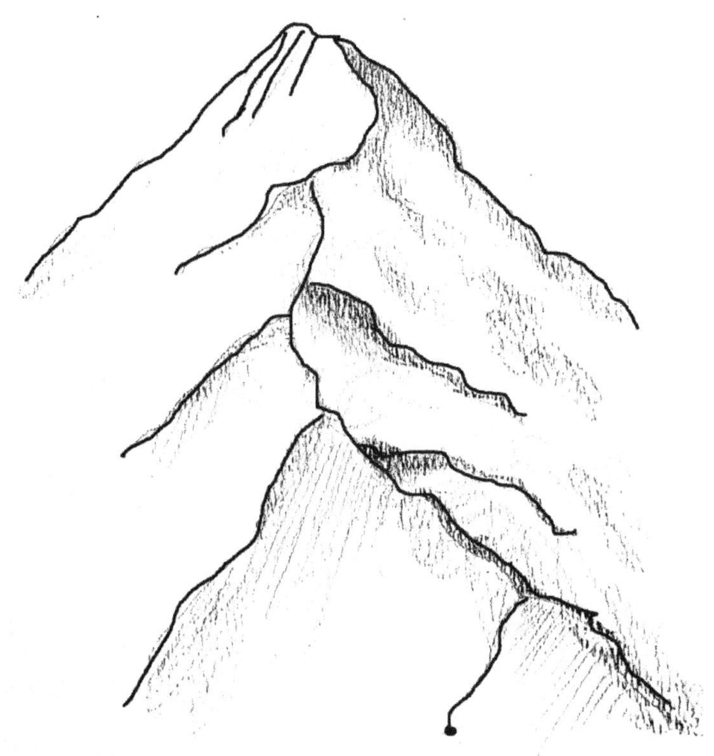

Week 5

Clouds with a Silver Lining: Why Do You Need Perspective?

Memory Verse

One of them, when he saw he was healed, came back, praising God in a loud voice.
(Luke 17:15 NIV)

Leadership Quality: Gratitude

Gratitude is the antidote for your fear, doubt, and disappointment.

Bible Story: Ten Lepers

Now on his way to Jerusalem, Jesus traveled along the border between Samaria and Galilee. As he was going into a village, ten men who had leprosy met him. They stood at a distance and called out in a loud voice, "Jesus, Master, have pity on us!"

When he saw them, he said, "Go, show yourselves to the priests." And as they went, they were cleansed.

One of them, when he saw he was healed, came back, praising God in a loud voice. He threw himself at Jesus' feet and thanked him—and he was a Samaritan.

Jesus asked, "Were not all ten cleansed? Where are the other nine? Has no one returned to give praise to God except this foreigner?" Then he said to him, "Rise and go; your faith has made you well." (Luke 17:11-19 NIV)

Day 1

Meditate

> One of them… (Luke 17:15 NIV)
>
> Jesus asked, "Were not all ten cleansed? Where are the other nine? 18 Has no one returned to give praise to God except this foreigner?" (Luke 17:17 NIV)

Observe

One is the loneliest number. I think there is a song about that. But in this case, ten men were grouped together yet alone and isolated from family, friends, and community. They knew what it meant to be lonely. These men had the disease that ate skin and limbs and left sores. Those who suffered from this serious skin disease had to tear their clothing and leave their hair uncombed. They had to cover their mouths and cry out, "Unclean! Unclean!" to warn people nearby (Lev. 13:35). They were labeled by society as lepers.

Leprosy created a horrific smell and progressed to the point of nerve damage. The disease was extremely contagious and offensive, robbing the person of all dignity. There was no known cure for leprosy. As Jesus was traveling to Jerusalem, the lepers saw Him and called out loudly and desperately to Him from a distance. After all, they had nothing to lose. No one knew of a leper being cured. The men were desperate for a miracle. Jesus simply told the men to show themselves to the priests, which the men immediately did.

Nevertheless, there was only one man, a Samaritan, who turned around and fell at Jesus' feet to thank Him. Only one person out of ten remembered to show gratitude about their miracle healing. One. Ten percent. Being a Samaritan is significant because people from Samaria were considered a dirty people group with whom not to associate. The Samaritan was the last person you would have expected to do the right and honorable thing. Have you ever felt like the Samaritan or the outcast? The one who everyone has low expectations of? It didn't matter to Jesus who the Samaritan was. It doesn't matter to Jesus what you have done. He loves Samaritans and you enough to heal and save you. Gratitude opens up doors for change of perspective and healing.

Repeat

I am loved, adored, and accepted by my Father in heaven.

Express

Lord, thank You.

Day 2

Meditate

> ...when he saw he was healed...
> (Luke 17:15 NIV)
>
> Trust in the Lord with all your heart
> and lean not on your own understanding;
> in all your ways submit to him,
> and he will make your paths straight.
> (Prov. 3:5-6 NIV)

Observe

A friend recently asked me, "How do you trust God?" Webster's definition of trust is to believe that someone is good and honest and will not harm you, or that something is safe and reliable. Trust is hoping and expecting that something is true. Trusting God allows you to live aware of the miracles going on around you right now, not just the ones you are waiting for. Trust and faith go hand in hand. Sometimes our mountains have clouds that prevent us from seeing the top. Clouds could be the times God does not reveal the end or the top of the mountain to save us from ourselves. God is teaching us to have more faith during these seasons. He gives us cloud cover to see only what's right in front of us so that we don't become self-sufficient and take any credit for any of the results ourselves.

We do not need to lean on our own understanding. We step out in faith trusting that God is going before us to smooth the path. Jesus told the men to go show themselves to the priests. Perhaps the men thought the priests would do the healing because the priests were the only ones able to declare their healing and freedom to enter back into the community. But when the Samaritan saw that he had already been healed on the way to the priests, he managed his miracle by thanking God. Thank God ahead of the answer, ahead of the miracle. Don't miss the miracles now by worrying about the future. Gratitude is an action, and the Samaritan's gratitude was loudly praising Jesus and falling at His feet. If only we could manage our everyday miracles with gratitude and praise! It is so important that we learn to fall at the right feet! Jesus' feet!

Repeat

I will trust You, Lord, in the clouds!

Express

I praise You, Lord! Thank You for being faithful. Thank You for Your trustworthiness. I thank You for the clouds. Build my faith and give me Your understanding and hope. I believe You are making my path straight. In Jesus' name, amen!

Day 3

Meditate

> ...came back... (Luke 17:15 NIV)

> Therefore confess your sins to each other and pray for each other so that you may be healed. The prayer of a righteous person is powerful and effective. (Jas. 5:16 NIV)

Observe

What are other reasons for clouds in our lives? One thing it could be is sin. Clouds can be dark and foreboding. Sin can create covers for hiding when we don't want to be found. But on the other side of these dark heavy clouds is hope and clear blue skies. One way we get this hope is through confession—yes, uncovering our clouds of sin. God wants us to confess these sins to Him and to others.

What freedom speaking the truth is! When we confess our sins, the heavens roar with freedom. The Samaritan came back and thanked Jesus. We have to come back every day and repent of our sins. Neither confession nor repentance is a single act that lasts a lifetime but a daily, sometimes hourly, act that keeps us close and open to the Holy

Spirit. Confessing and repenting of all your sins is freeing and healing because we no longer have to hold on to secrets or grudges. We get to unload all of our baggage and lighten our load. God doesn't mind that we have to come back to Him. He is there with arms wide open.

Repeat

> I confess my sins and the heavens roar with freedom!

Express

> Thank You for the power of confession and forgiveness. Convict me, Lord, when I need to confess my sins during the day even when I don't realize it. In Jesus' name, amen!

Day 4

Meditate

> ...praising God... (Luke 17:15 NIV)
>
> Praise him—he is your God, and you have seen with your own eyes the great and astounding things that he has done for you.
> (Deut. 10:21 GNT)

Observe

The Samaritan was praising God. The use of the word "praising" is continuous and never ceasing. It clears the clouds that can fill our minds to give us foggy thinking. Our to-do lists get so long and our minds become so cluttered. Whether it be sin or unclarity of thinking, we can choose to confess both and ask God for forgiveness and clarity. The Lord wants us to schedule margin and sabbath in our everyday life. We must protect our downtime because rest is meant for quiet time with Him through praising, praying, and reflecting.

Through rest and renewal, the clouds rise and clarity and creativity are given the freedom to be planted and grow. God-ideas and plans are given room to become a reality. Two questions can help filter your margin: Does this give me peace? What is the eternal value of saying yes to this situation? Praising becomes our fight song.

Repeat

> I will praise You while protecting our time together.

Express

> I praise you, Lord! Thank You for giving me clarity. Prepare my mind for action while being able to rest in You. You are my confident hope. In Jesus' name, amen!

Day 5

Meditate

…in a loud voice. (Luke 17:15 NIV)

In this you greatly rejoice, even though now for a little while, if necessary, you have been distressed by various trials, so that the proof of your faith, being more precious than gold which is perishable, even though tested by fire, may be found to result in praise and glory and honor at the revelation of Jesus Christ…
(1 Pet. 1:6-7 NASB)

Observe

As the fire devoured the salt, tamarind fruit, and brick dust, the gold became purer. The goldsmith took the gold out with tongs and, if it was not pure enough, he replaced it in the fire with a new mixture. But each time the gold was replaced, the heat was increased. The question was asked, "How do you know when the gold is purified?" The goldsmith answered, "When I can see my reflection in it" (Fort Washington, PA: Christian Literature Crusade, 1989). More of God's character is revealed when you are put in the fire.

During these times, we have a desperate need for a Savior. The only way to look is up. The only way to praise is loudly. We are changed to look and sound more and more like Jesus. There is purpose in the pain and reason to shout with a loud voice how much we love and praise Him for who He is and who we are in Him.

Repeat

I will trust Jesus in the fire and not be shaken.

Express

Lord, thank You for the fire and making me look more like You every day. Give me Your strength to withstand the heat and clean my heart. In Jesus' name, amen!

Days 6 & 7

MORE Reflection

> One of them, when he saw he was healed, came back, praising God in a loud voice.
> (Luke 17:15 NIV)

Why do you need perspective? Gratitude opens up our direction and focus to line up with Christ's perspective.

> Ascribe to the Lord, you heavenly beings,
> ascribe to the Lord glory and strength.
> Ascribe to the Lord the glory due his name;
> worship the Lord in the splendor of his holiness.
> The voice of the Lord is over the waters;
> the God of glory thunders,
> the Lord thunders over the mighty waters.
> The voice of the Lord is powerful;
> the voice of the Lord is majestic.
> The voice of the Lord breaks the cedars;
> the Lord breaks in pieces the cedars of Lebanon.
> He makes Lebanon leap like a calf,
> Sirion like a young wild ox.

The voice of the Lord strikes
  with flashes of lightning.
The voice of the Lord shakes the desert;
  the Lord shakes the Desert of Kadesh.
The voice of the Lord twists the oaks
  and strips the forests bare.
And in his temple all cry, "Glory!"
The Lord sits enthroned over the flood;
  the Lord is enthroned as King forever.
The Lord gives strength to His people;
  the Lord blesses His people with peace.
(Ps. 29 NIV)

Journal

What if we thanked God for the storms? Toward the end of Psalm 29, the lightning and thunder become a massive storm. The storm is so severe that the deer and oxen even give birth because they are so afraid. The trees are stripped bare of their leaves and limbs. But suddenly in the next verse, the picture of the calm after the storm takes over:

The Lord sits enthroned over the flood;
  the Lord is enthroned as King forever.
The Lord gives strength to His people;
  the Lord blesses His people with peace.
(Ps. 29:10-11 NIV)

His peace is the promise of a rainbow after the storm, after the chaos, after the struggle. This promise of peace comes in the New Testament as Jesus Christ. David didn't even know about Jesus yet. He just trusted God for full deliverance and freedom. The storms themselves are evidence of God's presence and provision. God is over all the storms. And He is the giver of peace in the middle of the storms as well as after.

The question we must ask ourselves is how will we allow our storms to create worship? Instead of allowing the storms to paralyze us, how can we find the motivation to remind ourselves that God is in control and working in the middle of the lightning and thunder? We can remember that Jesus came to rescue us. We can live in eager anticipation of Christ's return one day where we will be with Him for eternity in peace.

The biggest antidote for selfishness is the attitude of gratitude and serving others. Yes, you can even be grateful in struggles and hardships. My prayers start with everything that I am grateful for. Some days you have to start with little things. But you can always find something to be thankful for. Write a prayer in your journal and name at least three things you are thankful for today.

As a child, my favorite pastime was lying in the green grass and looking up to the blue sky with the big fluffy clouds. It was fun to use my imagination and make the clouds turn into different objects and stories with friends. Interestingly enough, everyone might see something different. Perspective is the same idea. In the following activities, keep in mind where we need to keep our focus so that our mountains stay small when we have God's perspective.

Create

We are experimenting with color this week. Color is the element of art that is produced when light, striking an object, is reflected back to the eye. There are three properties to color. The first is hue, which is simply the name we give to a color (red, yellow, blue, green, etc.). The second property is intensity, which refers to the vividness of the color. The third and final property of color is its value, meaning how light or dark it is.

Here are a few things to consider before you can run full speed ahead:

Watercolor Paints and Brushes:

Watercolor paints come in pans or tubes. A basic set will contain eight to ten colors. I prefer tube colors, but good quality pan colors are fine. Purchase student-grade or professional-grade watercolors. You will find that each artist has their own idea of what a basic set contains. This is my list of basic colors:

- new gamboge yellow
- yellow ocher
- burnt sienna
- sepia
- cadmium red
- alizarin crimson
- cerulean blue
- hookers green
- Payne's gray
- a neutral tint

Day 6 & 7

Recommended Brushes:

- #4 Round
- #8 Round
- #10 Round
- 1″ Flat Wash Brush

How Do I Use My Watercolor Supplies?

Before starting your first painting, it is important to become familiar with the way your paints, brushes, and paperwork together. I like to have two glasses of water, one to clean the paint off your brush and another with clean water. It is also a good idea to use painters' tape to attach your paper to a flat surface such as a cardboard or a wooden board you can lift. Practicing a few different methods on a scratch piece of watercolor paper will help you when you are aiming for different textures, smooth blending of colors, or a gradient of one color.

Let's practice ...

1. Set up your palette.

If you are using a plate, just squeeze a few colors on the edge. Space them far enough apart so they don't run together. If you have a palette with wells, you can squeeze each of your colors into individual wells.

2. Choose your colors.

- Choose three to five colors for your color palette.

- With a wet brush, pick up some of the paint and swirl it around in the center of your palette.
- Stroke a few strokes of paint onto a practice piece of scratch paper and try spreading it out to produce a gradient that goes from darker to lighter. Using more water with your color makes it lighter. A monochrome (one color) gradient is painted by using strong color at first and then adding water to thin and lighten the color. Since you do not add white to watercolors, you will get light colors by applying a thinner application of the same color.

3. What Techniques Do I Need to Know?

Here are a few basic techniques you should practice before attempting a painting:

*** Use the edge of a flat brush for sharp lines.**

Make sharp, dark lines with the edge of a 3/4" flat brush. This technique is excellent for grasses or deep, straight shadows. Load the edge of your brush with color and practice using the edge of the brush to make deep lines.

*** Paint textures with a dry brush technique.**

Painting with a fairly dry brush on dry paper is a great way to create rough textures. Heavily load a damp #10 round brush with a dark color. Use the brush on its side and pull it up along a tree trunk or a barn board. The paint will skip

Day 6 & 7

slightly, giving some very dark texture while leaving white highlights. Since you do not add white to watercolors, get light colors by applying more water to thin the application of the same color.

***Wet-on-Wet Wash Technique**

Wet your 2″ brush with clean water and cover the area of paper you want to paint. Then dab your color onto the wet paper and enjoy the blending of color. You can mix several colors but be careful to not get a muddy color, unless that's the look you are going for. You can pick up and tilt your paper to blend the colors.

***Wet-on-Dry Technique**

Painting on dry paper is a good way to get intense colors, detail, and texture in your work. As long as your brush does not have too much water on it, the paint will stay where you put it.

Try This Mountain Landscape Exercise:

1. Using painters' tape, attach your paper to a flat board that you can lift, such as cardboard. At any step in this painting, you may tilt your paper for the colors to blend.
2. We will be using a Wet-on-Wet Wash Technique. Using a large, 2″ flat wash brush, wash or cover the sky area with water. Spread it so the paper is wet, but make sure there aren't any puddles. You will need to

work quickly so the water does not dry before adding color.

3. Choose a sky color. For this exercise, I used cobalt blue. With a 1″ or 2″ flat brush, paint a smooth coat in the sky, darker at the top of the paper and lightening it up as you get to the horizon line.
4. Dip your dampened brush into a neutral tint or Payne's gray. Add a few cloudy areas. If your paper is still fairly damp, the gray will blend into the blue while still keeping the cloudy shapes. Don't overwork the sky or clouds. Once the color is on the paper, let the colors flow into one another for a natural, soft look. You may add a bit of new gamboge yellow, cadmium red, and burnt sienna for a sunrise/sunset sky.
5. Let the background dry naturally or quicken the process with a hair dryer before moving on.
6. After the sky is dry, repeat steps 1–5 with the mountain range. Feel free to use any color for your mountain range. All of our mountains will be different colors because we are each unique.

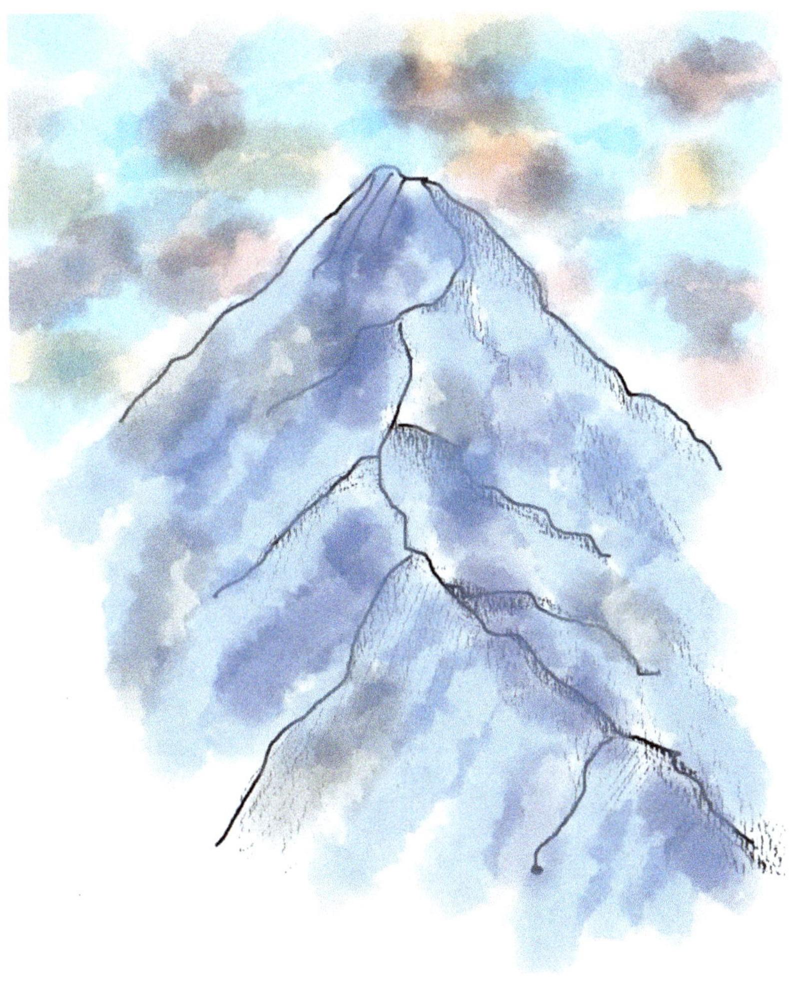

We will add to our mountain landscape next week.

Week 6

Mountain Climber's Packing List: How Do We Get Perspective?

Memory Verse for the Week:

> But Jesus said, "You feed them."
>
> "But we have only five loaves of bread and two fish," they answered. "Or are you expecting us to go and buy enough food for this whole crowd?" For there were about 5,000 men there.
>
> Jesus replied, "Tell them to sit down in groups of about fifty each." (Luke 9:13-14 NLT)

Leadership Trait: Delegation

Delegate tasks to spread the opportunity for blessings and relationships.

Bible Story: Feeding of the 5,000

One day Jesus called together his twelve disciples and gave them power and authority to cast out all demons and to heal all diseases. Then he sent them out to tell everyone about the Kingdom of God and to heal the sick. "Take nothing for your journey," he instructed them. "Don't take a walking stick, a traveler's bag, food, money, or even a change of clothes. Wherever you go, stay in the same house until you leave town. And if a town refuses to welcome you, shake its dust from your feet as you leave to show that you have abandoned those people to their fate."

So they began their circuit of the villages, preaching the Good News and healing the sick.

When Herod Antipas, the ruler of Galilee, heard about everything Jesus was doing, he was puzzled. Some were saying that John the Baptist had been raised from the dead. Others thought Jesus was Elijah or one of the other prophets risen from the dead.

"I beheaded John," Herod said, "so who is this man about whom I hear such stories?" And he kept trying to see him.

When the apostles returned, they told Jesus everything they had done. Then he slipped quietly away with them toward the town of Bethsaida. But the crowds found out where he was going, and they followed him. He welcomed them and taught them about the Kingdom of God, and he healed those who were sick.

Late in the afternoon the twelve disciples came to him and said, "Send the crowds away to the nearby villages and farms, so they can find food and lodging for the night. There is nothing to eat here in this remote place."

But Jesus said, "You feed them."

"But we have only five loaves of bread and two fish," they answered. "Or are you expecting us to go and buy enough food for this whole crowd?" For there were about 5,000 men there.

Jesus replied, "Tell them to sit down in groups of about fifty each." So the people all sat down. Jesus took the five loaves and two fish, looked up toward heaven, and blessed them. Then, breaking the loaves into pieces, he kept giving the bread and fish to the disciples so they could distribute it to the people. They all ate as much as they wanted, and afterward, the disciples picked up twelve baskets of leftovers!
(Luke 9 NLT)

Day 1

Meditate

> But Jesus said, "You feed them." (Luke 9:13 NLT)
>
> "Take nothing for your journey," he instructed them. "Don't take a walking stick, a traveler's bag, food, money, or even a change of clothes." (Luke 9:3 NLT)
>
> Do not conform to the pattern of this world, but be transformed by the renewing of your mind. Then you will be able to test and approve what God's will is—his good, pleasing and perfect will. (Rom. 12:2 NIV)

Observe

In our Bible story this week, there are really two stories in one passage. It begins with Jesus delegating His powerful authority to heal and deliver. Of course, the disciples were not the healers by themselves but healed in the name of Jesus. He also told them to take "nothing for the journey." Now, which one of us would even imagine taking a trip without even one or two of our favorite outfits or most comfortable shoes? On a mission trip to Madagascar, we were instructed to pack two weeks' worth of clothes and toiletries in a carry-on bag for the airplane. That's called creative packing. We learned all sorts of packing hacks to save room ... put your socks in your shoes, roll your clothes, recycle clothes.

It was the end of a long few days for the disciples of praying and preaching, trusting and traveling, when they all met back up with Jesus. The disciples were all looking forward to having some downtime with Jesus. Then the crowds showed up. The people had heard about the signs and wonders. Miraculous signs open doors as well as open ears, eyes, hearts, and minds to everything that God has for someone hungry for help and salvation.

When the 5,000-plus showed up hungry, interestingly enough, after Jesus told the disciples to take nothing for the journey, the disciples probably wanted to tell Jesus, "We knew we should have packed some snacks." And now Jesus tells them, "You feed them." During the day in Madagascar, teams of missionaries would travel the city doing street ministry and inviting the beautiful people to a festival at night in a huge stadium throughout the week. We went through the city "feeding" the people. These people would arrive at the festival hungry for change, aching to be different from the rest of the world.

Where are you getting fed? My spiritual father has a checklist of questions to ask each time he calls to check on me. The first thing he asks is, "Leesa, how is your vertical?" My question to you is the same, "How is *your* vertical? Are you reading your Word daily? Are you praying? Are you spending quality time with the Lord?" These questions are not meant to condemn but meant as a check to see if your heartline is vertical with God or horizontal with the world. When we focus on maintaining our vertical relationship with God, by abiding in Him, our horizontal relationships with others remain more harmonious and balanced too, because we are "In Christ." When things get out of whack with my horizontal relationships, I find it's because I have not remained plugged in to my source (Ps. 91:1-2).

Being connected to God is essential in your climb up the mountain. You are set apart by God for a special and unique purpose in this world. You have an assignment from a King. The world wants you to follow the world's plan, but you have been anointed to live differently than the world. You have been set apart.

Repeat

I am a world changer!

Express

Lord, help me to repeat my thinking to keep my focus and eyes on You. Help me to hold every thought captive and stay thinking about what You say. In Jesus' name, amen!

Day 2

Meditate

> "But we have only five loaves of bread and two fish," they answered. (Luke 9:13 NLT)
>
> So faith comes from hearing, that is, hearing the Good News about Christ. (Rom. 10:17 NLT)

Observe

The disciples were given the authority to heal and deliver. They would pray in Jesus' name while transforming the world. They were turning the world upside down in Jesus' name. After all the signs and wonders they had been performing, one would think that feeding a group of people would be an easy task. But they themselves were tired and hungry, and it was not a time to be making any important decisions. They were "hangry!"

When making important decisions, use the acronym **HALT**. Never make decisions when you are **H**ungry, **A**ngry, **L**onely, or **T**ired. The disciples were all four of these. They asked Jesus to send the people away under the disguise of being concerned about the people's hunger and rest when they really wanted to eat and sleep themselves.

Then Jesus simply said, "You feed them." That's all. Simple, right? They were with Jesus—the guy who heals the blind, the guy who raises the dead, the guy who drives demons out, puts them in pigs, and runs them off the cliff. Jesus makes it all look so simple. The disciples had seen and heard it all. But now when it comes to coming up with enough food, they panic. "But we have only five loaves of bread and two fish," they answered.

Through the years, I have discovered one of my spiritual gifts is hospitality. I love to cook to feed the thousands of teenagers and people who walk through my doors. I love people like Jesus through their stomachs. My husband bought me a beautiful oak table that seats ten one Christmas. My favorite thing is filling up every single seat at mealtime with enough food for seconds—just like the twelve baskets of leftovers, one basket for each disciple to pick up. And they were so concerned about the little amount of food at the beginning of the meal.

In Madagascar, we fed thousands of people with what little we had. At the same time, we were being fed by the joyful Malagasy people. But why do we think we have so little when God tells us that we are fearfully and wonderfully made? We are His masterpiece. We are the head and not the tail. We are set apart. The Malagasy people were so grateful to get fed with our "little." We saw so many signs and wonders in Africa.

After coming back home, I had such a hard time getting back into my world. My first-world daily problems, big and little, are hard to understand and superficial. My problems seem so small and insignificant compared to the needs He met so far away from my reality. I questioned why God wouldn't work things out like He did halfway around the world. We saw and experienced, firsthand, so many miracles of healing and deliverance. Why? How? I think the people were so desperately full of faith to see miracles. It's all done through praying in Jesus' name. He gives us more than enough to be His hands and feet. And He is not afraid of my questions.

The next thing my spiritual father would ask, "Leesa, are you praying with Kyle and the kids?" Sure, we all say we pray. We talk about praying and even tell others we'll pray for them. We have the best of intentions, but sometimes we use our prayer list as a gossip list, but do we actually pray? Do we call our friend about it before we go to God with it? And on top of that, do we pray out loud? Praying out loud is powerful because you can't fight with someone you are praying out loud with.

Romans 10:17 says, "So faith comes from hearing, that is, hearing the good news about Christ." Prayer is transforming. The power of prayer changes hearts and then situations. Most importantly, the heart change of prayer must happen before the outside circumstances change. Madagascar was a transforming experience that will forever change me and my family.

Repeat

I will show the world what Jesus looks like today.

Express

Father, thank You for being more than enough. Lord, check my heart today and wash it clean of anything holding me back from loving like You do. Come face to face with what I need to change. I surrender everything to You and want to be changed to look more like Jesus every day. In Jesus' name, amen!

Day 3

Meditate

> Or are you expecting us to go and buy enough food for this whole crowd? (Luke 9:13 NLT)
>
> But the fruit of the Spirit is love, joy, peace, forbearance, kindness, goodness, faithfulness, gentleness and self-control. Against such things there is no law. (Gal. 5:22-23 NIV)

Observe

The next question on my packing list is, "Are you practicing the fruit of the Spirit (peace, love, joy, patience, kindness, goodness, faithfulness, gentleness, and self-control ... Galatians 5:22)?" Ouch. The Holy Spirit gives us the Fruit of the Spirit, and each one grows over time. The fruit of the Spirit are all traits that are fulfilled in a restful soul. Busyness and chaos are not conducive to showing peace, love, and joy. Being critical does not hold hands with patience, kindness, and goodness. Selfishness is not excited about being faithful, gentle, or having self-control.

Being filled with all these traits will change your perspective because you are focusing on God and being led by the Holy Spirit. After Jesus had preached, healed, and fed, He released the people and the disciples to go and rest. Jesus then went up on the mountainside to pray. Resting renews our minds. Studies have shown that the main difference that makes maestro violinists who they are is not only the amount of practice time but their sleep time. They get a quality eight hours of sleep, at least, which turns to quality practice time full of focus and concentration. Sleep and rest heal our body and mind. Jesus does expect us to renew our mind by spending time in the Word, which calms and renews. Finding those verses that reach the bottom of your heart will ripen that fruit.

Repeat

I will think about what I'm thinking about and will repeat it to line up with God's Word.

Express

Lord, thank You for filling me with Your love, joy, peace, patience, kindness, goodness, faithfulness, gentleness, and self-control. Lead me by Your Spirit today. In Jesus' name, amen!

Day 4

Meditate

> For there were about 5,000 men there.
> (Luke 9:14 NLT)
>
> For even the Son of Man did not come expecting to be served by everyone, but to serve everyone, and to give his life as the ransom price in exchange for the salvation of many.
> (Mark 10:45 TPT)

Observe

Finally, on my checklist, I am reminded that I should only use my words to "edify, build-up, and encourage" others. Jesus constantly spoke encouragement and life into others. God's will is for us to speak life, be a light on a hill, and be the salt of the earth. During our time in Shreveport, my family got the opportunity to serve at a local homeless ministry, The Hub. The urban ministry was the hangout shelter for people to get fed physically, spiritually, and artistically. My husband led a spiritual leadership class, and I taught an art class with a friend weekly. What a privilege and honor it was to love and encourage those sweet people.

As the disciples served the food to the 5000-plus people, including men, women, and children, they were able to encourage and build up the people. This time of hunger and serving became a time of building relationships and connections. We want to be a light in our little part of the world and put on the full armor of God before going into the world for the day. Isn't that what Jesus asked us to do?

Repeat

> I will build up, encourage, and edify others today.

Express

> Thank You for Your plan and purpose for my life. Make me Your mouthpiece speaking life into others today. In Jesus' name, amen!

Day 5

Meditate

> Jesus replied, "Tell them to sit down in groups of about fifty each." (Luke 9:14 NLT)
>
> Finally, brothers and sisters, whatever is true, whatever is noble, whatever is right, whatever is pure, whatever is lovely, whatever is admirable—if anything is excellent or praiseworthy—think about such things. (Phil. 4:8 NIV)

Observe

We often get caught up in knowing what God's will is. Then He reminds me of the Faith Formula ... Word + Prayer + Fellowship. These three things are ways God speaks to us and are so important in living an abundant life. God talks to us through His Word. The Bible is a living book because the same verse you read this time last year may speak to you in a different way because you are in a different season and circumstance this year.

Prayer is a conversation between you and God. Fellowship with other believers helps us to grow and be comforted. Life gets messy sometimes. We need the Word, prayer, and fellowship to help us through these rough spots and messes. A good analogy of finding yourself in the middle of a mess is being in a car wreck and the car still flipping in the air. We all know the car will land but won't know yet if there will be any casualties. Sure, there would be bumps and bruises, and possibly some broken bones, but all of these injuries can be mended and healed by God. At this point is where the healing process begins. Complete healing is forgiving those who have wronged you and loving your enemies.

Jesus organized and delegated the feast, from finding the food, seating the guests, and sharing the fish and bread. God orders our steps and our healing. When we see that God is using every circumstance for His glory, we understand and accept the outcomes easier. God wants to take over and give you His rest. He is faithful and wants us to keep our eyes on Him. Keep your mind on the right things, pure things, lovely things, admirable things, excellent and praiseworthy things.

Repeat

I will keep my focus on God today!

Express

Thank You, Lord, for being faithful even when I am not. Help me to know Your true and perfect will by bringing Scripture to mind all through the day. Order my steps today. In Jesus' name, amen!

Days 6 & 7

MORE Reflection

> He replied, "You give them something to eat."
>
> They answered, "We have only five loaves of bread and two fish—unless we go and buy food for all this crowd." (About five thousand men were there.)
>
> But he said to his disciples, "Have them sit down in groups of about fifty each."
> (Luke 9:13-14 NIV)

How do you get perspective? Delegation allows you to share in serving with others to see through Jesus' eyes. Perspective requires delegation of our priorities of serving others and gratitude over our selfish nature. Some theologians suggest there might have been as many as 20,000 people there, including women and children. The world does not revolve around your belly button. Jesus modeled serving others so that we too would serve others.

> Finally, brothers and sisters, whatever is true, whatever is noble, whatever is right, whatever is pure, whatever is lovely, whatever is admirable—if anything is excellent or praiseworthy—think about such things. (Phil. 4:8 NIV)

Journal

If you are in a valley, remember the good times, the times you could laugh about, the sweet memories. It can't be all bad. There must be some good times in there somewhere. Keep in mind that this season is just a comma in your life. Sometimes God encourages us to slow down and look at our environment or situation and compare it to what is inside of us. Remember the fruit is grown in the valleys. Journal about these good times.

Create

This week, we will be using the element of space to add trees to our drawing. In art, space is the area around the object you are drawing. Space can be negative or positive, just like our thoughts. It shows depth to our objects in many different ways. It can be overlapping the objects, and the size of the object in the drawing is larger when close and smaller when far away. The color of the object gets lighter the further away the object gets. Perspective is also a way to create space in relation to the horizon line. A few things to ask yourself as you plan your drawing: Do you want to use overlapping, create positive or negative space, or use color or perspective in your drawing? There are a few examples included, but feel free to do your own thing.

1. We will be drawing trees today. The simpler the better because you will be drawing these shapes many times around your paper in different sizes, which creates variety. Repeating shapes creates unity.
2. In planning the placement of your trees, divide your paper, in your mind, into thirds, horizontally and vertically. Artists have a rule of thirds that make your composition more interesting to your viewer. You want to place objects close to where the lines intersect.

3. There are two ways to insert trees into your piece. With your pencil, lightly and loosely sketch trees on your drawing. Or you may use your brush to directly add trees to your art. If you choose the brush, practice on your scratch paper. Add a few clusters of tree trunks along the horizon. Plan on having background trees, midline trees, and trees in the foreground. Begin with the background

trees and work forward to the foreground trees. The closer you get to the foreground trees, the ones closest to the viewer, the darker, larger, and more detailed they will need to be. The background trees are less detailed, smaller, and lighter in color. Space can be achieved by overlapping the objects and adjusting the size of the object in the drawing to be larger when close and smaller when far away.

4. For the foreground trees, use a natural tint on a round brush that is fairly heavy and dry; roughly paint in a tree trunk and some branches and leaves.
5. Using a small brush and grey paint, carefully outline your mountain and its ridges. Painting on dry paper is a good way to get intense colors, detail, and texture in your work. As long as your brush does not have too much water on it, the paint will stay where you put it. You can use very tiny brushes to add fine detail or larger ones to create texture in wood or trees.
6. Using your small brush and gray paint, add value to your mountain to make it more realistic. Begin with more water on your brush with your paint. It is easier to start lighter and layer your colors for darker or more value. Always test your color on your swatch paper.
7. When you paint some foliage on the tree, wet irregular areas where the leaves will go and

drop in some bits of yellow ocher and green in the branches and on the ground.

8. While the paper and color are still wet, add some areas of cadmium red and sap green. The colors should flow together slightly.
9. If you intend to paint a soft background behind a mountain or tree with a lot of texture, be sure to do that first with a wet-on-wet technique. Your background should be perfectly dry before starting on the textured areas—otherwise, they will run.

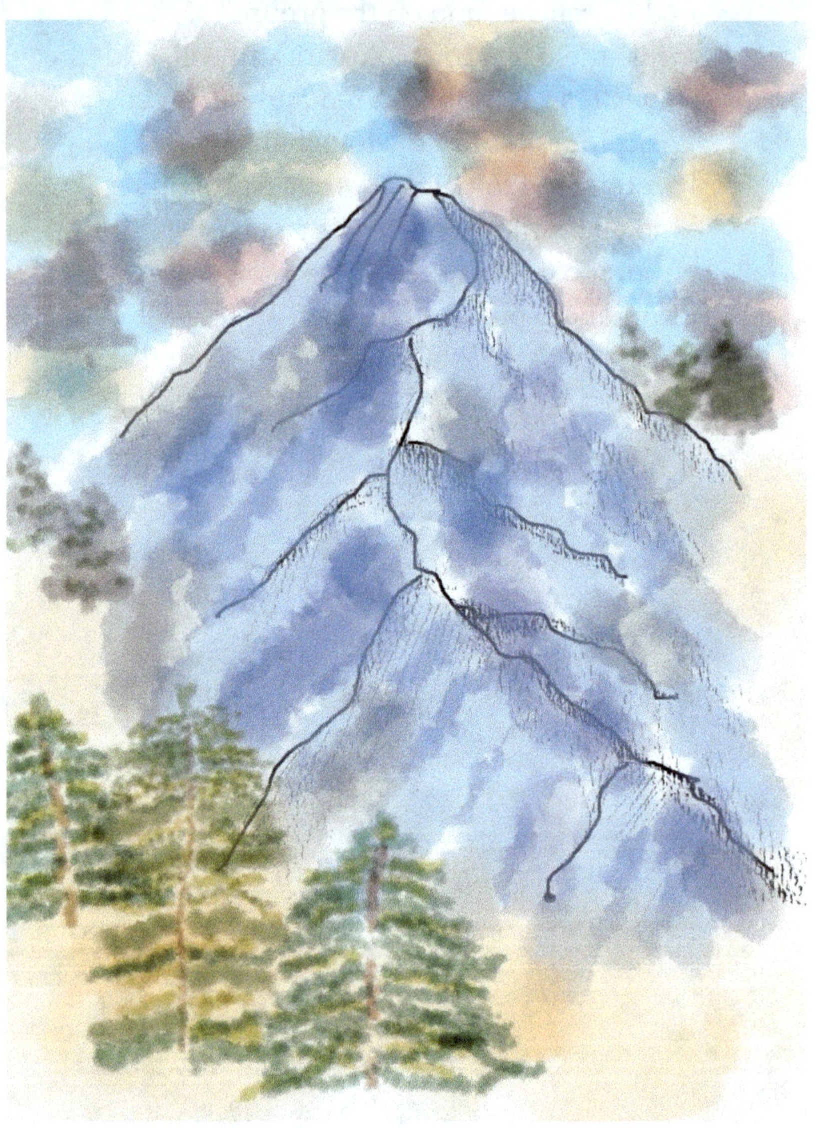

Your masterpiece is almost complete. Let's bravely climb our mountain to our high place next week.

Week 7

BRAVE Blessing

Memory Verse for the Week

Then David accepted from her hand what she had brought him and said, "Go home in peace. I have heard your words and granted your request." (1 Sam. 25:35 NIV)

Leadership Trait: Connection

Connection is being humble enough to build relationships and touch hearts that need and long to be noticed.

Bible Story: Abigail

A certain man in Maon, who had property there at Carmel, was very wealthy. He had a thousand goats and three thousand sheep, which he was shearing in Carmel. **3** His name was Nabal and his wife's name was Abigail. She was an intelligent and beautiful woman, but her husband was surly and mean in his dealings—he was a Calebite.

While David was in the wilderness, he heard that Nabal was shearing sheep. So he sent ten young men and said to them, "Go up to Nabal at Carmel and greet him in my name. Say to him: 'Long life to you! Good health to you and your household! And good health to all that is yours!

"'Now I hear that it is sheep-shearing time. When your shepherds were with us, we did not mistreat them, and the whole time they were at Carmel nothing of theirs was missing. Ask your own servants and they will tell you. Therefore be favorable toward my men, since we come at a festive time. Please give your servants and your son David whatever you can find for them.'"

When David's men arrived, they gave Nabal this message in David's name. Then they waited.

Nabal answered David's servants, "Who is this David? Who is this son of Jesse? Many servants are breaking away from their masters these days. Why should I take my bread and water, and the meat I have slaughtered for my shearers, and give it to men coming from who knows where?"

David's men turned around and went back. When they arrived, they reported every word. David said to his men, "Each of you strap on your sword!" So they did, and David strapped his on as well. About four hundred men went up with David, while two hundred stayed with the supplies.

One of the servants told Abigail, Nabal's wife, "David sent messengers from the wilderness to give our master his greetings, but he hurled insults at them. Yet these men were very good to us. They did not mistreat us, and the whole time we were out in the fields near them nothing was missing. Night and day they were a wall around us the whole time we were herding our sheep near them. Now think it over and see what you can do, because disaster is hanging over our master and his whole household. He is such a wicked man that no one can talk to him."

Abigail acted quickly. She took two hundred loaves of bread, two skins of wine, five dressed sheep, five seahs of roasted grain, a hundred cakes of raisins and two hundred cakes of pressed figs, and loaded them on donkeys. Then she told her servants, "Go on ahead; I'll follow you." But she did not tell her husband Nabal.

As she came riding her donkey into a mountain ravine, there were David and his men descending toward her, and she met them. David had just said, "It's been useless—all my watching over this fellow's property in the wilderness so that nothing of his was missing. He has paid me back evil for good. May God deal with David, be it ever so severely, if by morning I leave alive one male of all who belong to him!"

When Abigail saw David, she quickly got off her donkey and bowed down before David with her face to the ground. She fell at his feet and said: "Pardon your servant, my lord, and let me speak to you; hear what your servant has to say. Please pay no attention, my lord, to that wicked man Nabal. He is just like his name—his name means Fool, and folly goes with him. And as for me, your servant, I did not see the men my lord sent. And now, my lord, as surely as the Lord your God lives and as you live, since the Lord has kept you from bloodshed and from avenging yourself with your own hands, may your enemies and all who are intent on harming my lord be like Nabal. And let this gift, which your servant has brought to my lord, be given to the men who follow you.

"Please forgive your servant's presumption. The Lord your God will certainly make a lasting dynasty for my lord, because you fight the Lord's battles, and no wrongdoing will be found in you as long as you live. Even though someone is pursuing you to take your life, the life of my lord will be bound securely in the bundle of the living by the Lord your God, but the lives of your enemies he will hurl away as from the pocket of a sling. When the Lord has fulfilled for my lord every good thing he promised concerning him and has appointed him ruler over Israel, my lord will not have on his conscience the staggering burden of needless bloodshed or of having avenged himself. And when the Lord your God has brought my lord success, remember your servant."

David said to Abigail, "Praise be to the Lord, the God of Israel, who has sent you today to meet me. May you be blessed for your good judgment and for keeping me from bloodshed this day and from avenging myself with my own hands. Otherwise, as surely as the Lord, the God of Israel, lives, who has kept me from harming you, if you had not come quickly to meet me, not one male belonging to Nabal would have been left alive by daybreak."

Then David accepted from her hand what she had brought him and said, "Go home in peace. I have heard your words and granted your request."

When Abigail went to Nabal, he was in the house holding a banquet like that of a king. He was in high spirits and very drunk. So she told him nothing at all until daybreak. Then in the morning, when Nabal was sober, his wife told him all these things, and his heart failed him and he became like a stone. About ten days later, the Lord struck Nabal and he died. (1 Sam. 25:2-38 NIV)

Day 1

Meditate

> Then David accepted from her hand…
> (1 Sam. 25:35 NIV)
>
> Wait for the Lord;
> be strong and take heart
> and wait for the Lord. (Ps. 27:14 NIV)

Observe

Have you ever been in a relationship where you felt like you needed to apologize and make amends for the other person to those around you? Do you ever feel like you are put in the middle of sticky situations and conversations because you are seen as the one who is rational and reasonable? You must have the leadership quality of connection. You can see the big picture and break it into smaller pieces to solve the problem.

In the same way, Abigail in our story was a woman of beauty, brilliance, and benevolence. She had the wisdom to see the 30,000-foot view and then come down the mountain to meet David and make the connection on his path to destruction and demise. In David's volatile situation of anger and testosterone, Abigail found her strength from the Lord. While David and his men were strapping on their armor and weapons, Abigail was gathering raisins and fig bread to appease David's gang. Before gathering the raisin bread, she gathered the Lord's strength to gather a feast before Nabal noticed what she was doing.

Her prayer that morning probably went something like this, "Lord, give me Your strength today to be a peacemaker. Make me strong in You, today. Help me to wait on You and make connections today. Please guide me and go before me today, Lord, prepare in advance the hearts of those I talk to, and give me Your peace and Your favor today."

Abigail's peacemaker perspective of the situation caused her to humble herself before David. She wanted to protect her husband and her household from death, prevent rash regrets from David, and provide a secure future for herself. Each player in this story had a different perspective, but only one character had God's. Abigail was a brave connector.

As our children were growing up, I felt the nudge to write a "BRAVE Blessing." In today's BRAVE Blessing, the letter B stands for "Bold." You are bold and confident in Christ. Philippians 1:20b (NLT) says, "I will continue to be bold for Christ." I love the word *continue* because it means you have been bold in the past and choose to be bold in your future—bold to stand firm in your faith and beliefs when the world around you says and does the opposite, bold to wait on the Lord's timing. Beginning your day with the idea of being Brave to go into the world as a mighty warrior for the Lord is so important for us grownups and especially for our kids.

You are BRAVE! Remember who and Whose you are!

Repeat

I am bold in Christ.

Express

Lord, You are the Light of the world. Thank You for making me be a light that reflects Your love and truth. Help me to continue to be bold for You. Lord, give me Your strength today to be a peacemaker. Make me strong in You today. Help me to wait on You. Make me Bold. In Jesus' name, amen!

Day 2

Meditate

> ...what she had brought him...
> (1 Sam. 25:35 NIV)
>
> I can do all things through Christ who strengthens me. (Phil. 4:13 NKJV)
>
> My dear brothers and sisters, take note of this: Everyone should be quick to listen, slow to speak and slow to become angry...
> (Jas 1:19 NIV)

Observe

Today's letter in BRAVE is R for "Ready." James 1:19 (MSG) says, "Post this at all the intersections, dear friends: Lead with your ears, follow up with your tongue, and let anger straggle along in the rear." Being quick and leading is being ready. Being ready is a call to action, being ready to help. Firemen are ready to rush to the fire. Athletes are ready to compete. People get ready in the mornings to go to work or school.

Anytime my kids had to be ready for a challenge in front of them, I would remind them to say the "Ten Fingers" ... "I can (fill in the blank with "ace the test, hit the ball, tell the truth") through Christ who strengthens me." It reminds them that Christ is beside you, before you, behind you, and, most importantly, inside you to help you and never leave or forsake you. 1 Peter 3:15 says, "Instead, you must worship Christ as Lord of your life. And if someone asks about your hope as a believer, always be ready to explain it." Be ready to share what God has done in you and for you.

James tells us to be quick and ready to listen. Listening doesn't require movement, but there should be a sense of urgency. We need the Lord's strength to stop and listen. Sometimes the only thing someone needs is to be heard. Be a listener who doesn't feel the need to fix. Just listen with grace and understanding. Listen to both sides, remembering there are always two sides to every story. Empathetically, see the situation through the other person's eyes, and put yourself in their shoes. Stopping to listen gives us time to pray and hear from God. Listening to God to get His guidance and perspective requires us to be still. Being ready means being still to listen.

Repeat

> I am ready to listen first to God and others today.

Express

Lord, thank You for always listening to me. Help me to stop and listen to You so that I may be obedient. Give me Your strength to open my ears today and take the time to listen. In Jesus' name, amen!

Day 3

Meditate

> ...and said, "Go home in peace..."
> (1 Sam. 25:35 NIV)
>
> Rejoice always, pray continually, give thanks in all circumstances; for this is God's will for you in Christ Jesus. (1 Thess. 5:16-18 NIV)

Observe

The letter A in BRAVE stands for always. You are always rejoicing and giving thanks to God in everything. EVERYTHING! Pray about everything. God is Good ALL the time ... even in your good and bad days!" What? You can thank God in the struggling seasons, the chaotic circumstances, the terrifying times? Yes, you can, because you can trust that He is working in the middle of it all. Remember and be thankful for His faithfulness.

Notice it says *in* everything not *for* everything. We can still have His joy and hope *in* everything, but not everything is good. While you wait for the Lord, pray about everything and trust that He is doing more than you can see. He has already worked it out because He goes before us.

He is not surprised at anything, and nothing is wasted. Trust that His timing is perfect. Everything in our lives is either caused or allowed by God. We just need to hurry up and wait for the Lord. He is Sovereign and so worthy to be praised. We can praise and give thanks to God in everything that comes our way because He promises to work everything out for the good of those who love Him and are called for His purpose. The "good" will always give God the glory. He will give you peace beyond understanding. Oftentimes, I pray to remind myself, and God, of his faithful promises.

Repeat

I will *always* rejoice in everything!

Express

Lord, I thank and praise You in the good and the bad. I know that You are in control and will work it out for the good. I love You, Lord. In Jesus' name, amen!

Day 4

Meditate

> I have heard your words… (1 Sam. 25:35 NIV)
>
> When the angel of the Lord appeared to Gideon, he said, "The Lord is with you, mighty warrior." (Judg. 6:12 NIV)

Observe

Today, V stands for Valiant. You are a Valiant and Mighty Warrior in the name of the Lord, with humility, generosity, and integrity. You are fearfully and wonderfully made. God says that He will give me His strength to walk through any storm or fire. He calls me valiant and mighty. At the same time, He wants me to remain humble and honest with others and myself. Be generous with others, expecting nothing in return. Being Brave can also mean being Vulnerable to be real to ask for help and prayers. Being Brave is being real. It's OK not to be OK. And sometimes we must encourage ourselves and talk to those fears.

Abigail listened to the servants tell about the encounter with Nabal and David's men. David listened and considered what Abigail brought him on the road. Abigail not only brought food, but she brought peace and perspective. The act of listening in this story prompted action for peace and prevention from destruction. Abigail did not let her fear of David's anger outweigh the need for action to make amends. David did not let his anger control his need to listen and reconsider. There are several examples in the Bible where God changes his mind, but he never changes his character. Listening is a skill that helps make that connection with others possible for reconciliation.

Abigail waited on the Lord to handle her husband. She guarded her heart and mouth by not lashing out toward her husband in anger. Instead, she was humbly generous and asked for forgiveness. The Lord honors our waiting because we are trusting His hand is always moving. Often, valiant warriors are most effective when they are still and quiet.

Repeat

I am a valiant and mighty warrior for Him!

Express

Lord, thank You for Your presence. I can do all things through Your strength.

Day 5

Meditate

> ...and granted your request. (1 Sam. 25:35 NIV)

> So encourage each other and build each other up, just as you are already doing. (1 Thess. 5:11 NLT)

Observe

In BRAVE, the letter E stands for Encouraging and Edifying. You are Encouraging, Edifying, and Building up others while practicing the fruit of the Spirit—peace, joy, love, patience, kindness, goodness, humility, faithfulness, and self-control. Do BRAVE out loud as often as you can. Your family needs to hear you speak Blessings to them and over them even when their eyes roll and sighs come. You can shorten and give them the nitty-gritty version—something like, "You are BRAVE. Remember who and Whose you are. You are Bold, Ready, Always Rejoicing, Valiant, and Encouraging ... and don't you forget it!"

Your BRAVE Blessing is your Fight Song for your kids or anyone else who needs to hear it from you! Let's be the ones to speak life into others and not wait for others to speak into us. I challenge you to say this Blessing, or create your own, to those around you. If you were to write your own blessing, what would it be?

Repeat

I will speak life into others today.

Express

Lord, thank You for your encouragement every day. Help me to lift up others with words that speak life. Show me who to encourage today with a smile, a word, or an action that shows them Jesus. In Jesus' name, amen!

Days 6 & 7

MORE Reflection

I will give thanks to You, for I am fearfully and
wonderfully made;
Wonderful are Your works,
and my soul knows it very well.
(Ps. 139:14 NASB)

Journal

Perspective changes when connection is made and hearts are open.

"Are you awake?" "You have 10 minutes before the Mom bus leaves!" "Make time for Breakfast." These are all things heard around our house in the mornings before school. About three years ago, the Lord put the BRAVE Blessing on my heart to declare and pray over my children every day. I don't know who started the old saying, "Sticks and stones may break my bones, but words will never hurt me," but it is the most untrue statement there is. Our words are seeds that we plant into others. The seeds will either rot the listener or produce a beautiful flower. Our words speak life or death to our listeners. Let someone know today they can be the bold Light in the world.

- I am Bravely Beautiful inside and out.
- I will not be shaken. I'm Yours today.
- I am Brave to be Bold and confident in Christ.
- Brave to be Ready to listen, slow to speak, and slow to anger.
- Brave to Always be thankful in everything.
- Brave to be a Valiant and mighty warrior for the Lord, yet Vulnerable to be real.
- Brave to be Encouraging to others.
- BRAVE to love and create!

Create

Our journey ends with the element of shape. To add shape to your mountain piece, you may choose to add an eagle, the word "Brave," or your favorite verse. You are invited to write out the given Brave Blessing in your journal or create your own unique Blessing to speak out loud for you and others who need an encouraging word.

If you choose to write on your picture, you may use hand lettering, which is a form of art that imitates calligraphy. The beauty comes in the pressure you put on your pen for the upstrokes and downstrokes of the letters. The downstrokes are heavier pressure and thicker marks. The upstrokes of the letters are less pen pressure and thinner marks. The following example shows you how to hand-letter the word "Brave."

Step 1: Hand-letter the word in pencil on a practice sheet.

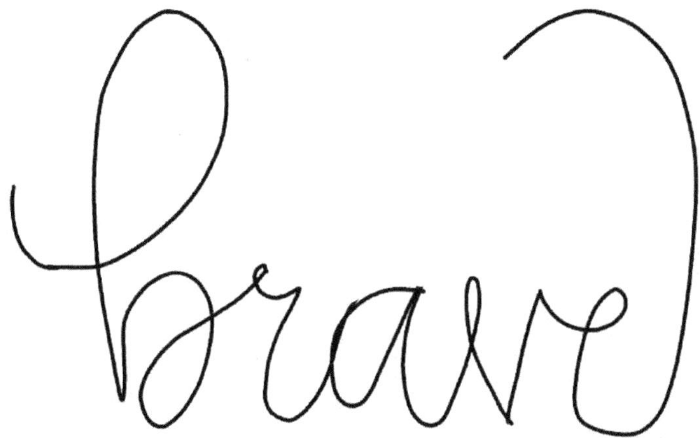

Step 2: Double the lines on the downstrokes of your letters, still in pencil.

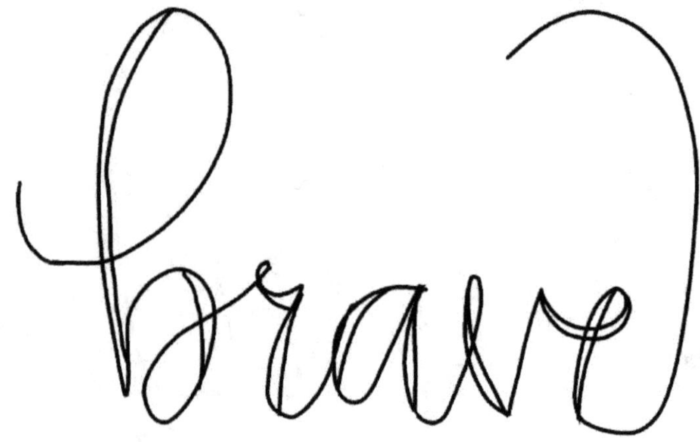

Step 3: Using a marker pen, trace your word, making the downstrokes heavier and darker than the upstrokes on the letters. I like to use the black Tombow, Fudenosuke, or the Sharpie pen.

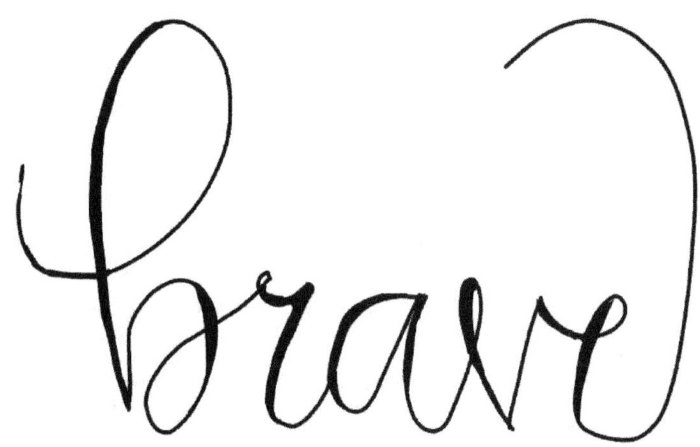

After you get comfortable practicing the word, you may decide to place it on your mountain scene drawing. I would love to see your masterpiece. You can post it under the hashtag #whatcolorisyourmountain. You are graced forward to be brave.

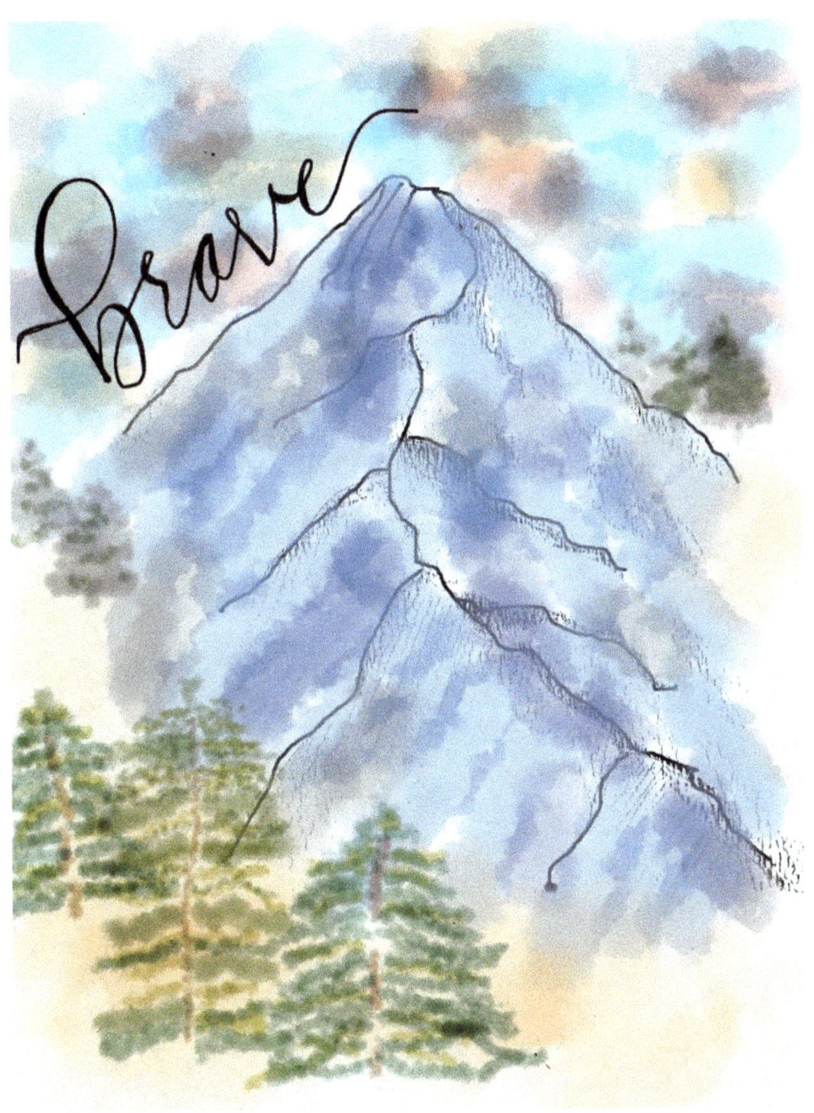

Enjoy the climb, warrior.

www.ingramcontent.com/pod-product-compliance
Lightning Source LLC
LaVergne TN
LVHW020055110826
845155LV00022B/85